Diabetic Cookbook for Beginners UK 2021

Diabetic Recipe Book with Delicious and Simple Diabetes Type 1 & Type 2 Recipes with a 21 Day Meal Plan and Blood Sugar Diary.

Sarah Jones

Table of Contents

Hey there!

I would like to thank you for your trust and I really hope you'll enjoy the book.

A lot of thought and effort went into creating the book. I am not a part of a big publishing company and I take care of the whole publishing process myself in an effort to make sure your cooking journey is as smooth as possible.

If for any reason you did not like the book you can write on my email at deliciousrecipes.publishing@gmail.com. I always make sure to get back to everybody and if you're not happy with the book I can share another book.

I'm trying really hard to create the best cookbooks I can and I'm always open to constructive criticism.

Enjoy!

Diabetes Fundamentals – Everything You Need To Know To Start Improving Your Condition

You may already understand some of the basics of diabetes, but just in case, we'll briefly cover the fundamental causes. Diabetes is a condition where the level of glucose in your blood is too high. This occurs because your body is not producing any insulin, or at least not sufficient amounts to regulate the glucose levels. Type 1 diabetes is when you are unable to make any insulin at all, and type 2 is when you can produce insulin, but not in sufficient quantities, or it doesn't work effectively. Diabetes is a very serious condition, but with proper management, you can get type 2 diabetes under control and even into remission without having to depend on medication. Eating well and exercising frequently are the keys to handling type 2 diabetes without medication, but the condition can get progressively worse, and it needs to be monitored by health professionals to ensure that it remains under control. Medication may be needed at the later stages to prevent the diabetes from having a negative impact on the rest of the body.

You will still need to eat well and stay fit in order to manage diabetes effectively, even if you take medication.

What Is An A1C Test?

To be diagnosed as diabetic, you must undergo an A1C test. This is a blood test that is used to diagnose type 2 diabetes and prediabetes. It measures how much of the **haemoglobin** in your blood is coated with sugar. A high percentage indicates a high glucose level, which suggests that you may be at risk of type 2 diabetes.

Someone who has high glucose levels but is not yet at the point of being diabetic may be diagnosed as prediabetic. If your glucose level is between 5.7% and 6.4%, you are usually considered prediabetic. Above 5.7% is considered type 2 diabetic.

Your A1C level is your three-month average blood sugar level.

The Latest Scientific Research On Diabetes

Research is constantly being done on what causes diabetes and how we can better treat it. The focus has been moving toward getting type 2 diabetes into remission, rather than using medicines to treat it where possible.

This often involves weight loss and careful dietary management systems. At present, type 2 diabetes is around 24 times more common than type 1, and thus a lot of focus is placed upon dealing with it. The treatment so far has tended to try and deal with the symptoms of diabetes, i.e. the increased blood glucose levels. Now, however, scientists[1] are beginning to look at how obesity and fatty liver disease are connected with and could contribute to type 2 diabetes. Studies are being done on how the liver can affect insulin sensitivity, and whether fat in the liver can contribute to diabetes or cause the body to become more resistant to insulin.

This study found that a fatty liver increases production of a neurotransmitter called Gamma-aminobutyric acid (GABA), which is the main inhibitory transmitter in the central nervous system. Decreased nerve activity reduces the communication between the brain and body tissues. The study found that inhibiting excess GABA production in animal models restored insulin sensitivity in a small amount of time. More study is needed to understand whether this could translate to humans, but it is hoped that better understanding the relationship between obesity and diabetes will massively improve the available treatments in the coming years.

Many scientists are also looking into the possibility that supplements could help to manage or even possibly prevent diabetes. Certain supplements may be capable of lowering blood sugar levels to an extent, and if so, they can help to deal with the same symptom that most medications are currently addressing. It is not thought that supplements are sufficient to get diabetes sufferers off medication entirely, but they may help reduce the need for medication, and help treat prediabetes.

In the next chapter, we'll cover some of the supplements that may be able to help people handle diabetes. Remember, these are not a substitute for medical advice; if you are concerned about your health, you should seek the guidance of a certified medical professional. Supplements may help you to be healthier, but they should not be used to replace prescribed medication or as an alternative to seeing a healthcare professional.

---

1   University of Arizona. "A promising new pathway to treating type 2 diabetes." ScienceDaily. ScienceDaily, 29 June 2021. <www.sciencedaily.com/releases/2021/06/210629191737.htm>.

Powerful Diabetes Supplement Stack To Manage Diabetes

So, what supplements have so far been related to diabetes and how might they be able to help? Adjusting your diet to include these foods or taking supplements is a great way to manage diabetes and prediabetes, although you should always consult your doctor before making drastic changes to your diet.

The following information has been taken from the Healthline website[2]. It is correct as of 1/08/2021.

1) Cinnamon

Cinnamon can be used in your food or taken as a supplemental tablet. It is thought to lower blood sugar, which can help control diabetes. Taking 250 mg of cinnamon two times a day can decrease your blood sugar levels when fasting, and can also lower the **haemoglobin** A1C.

2) American Ginseng

A variant of ginseng grown in North America has been shown to bring down blood sugar levels following a meal by around 20% both for individuals with type 2 diabetes and for individuals who are not diabetic or prediabetic. It is thought that ginseng both increases the insulin production and improves the cell response to insulin.

A gram of ginseng can be taken up to two hours before a meal, but should not be taken further from a meal as it can cause a dip in blood sugar. Do not take ginseng if you are on warfarin or immunosuppressant drugs.

3) Probiotics

Probiotics are also thought to help regular the blood sugar levels of people who regularly consume them. Probiotics contain beneficial microbes that can improve how your body deals with carbohydrates.

If your probiotics are varied and contain several different kinds of bacteria, they can have an even greater impact on your fasting blood sugar levels, so try to choose probiotics that have several different kinds of microbes in them. This will give you the best results.

4) Aloe Vera

The juice of the aloe vera plant could also help to lower fasting blood sugar levels, as could supplements from the plant. Studies done on mice have indicated that taking aloe vera could possibly increase the ability of pancreatic cells to produce insulin. This needs further study to be confirmed.

Supplementing with aloe may help with both type 2 diabetes and prediabetes, but so far, a dose hasn't been recommended by medical sources. Some of the doses tested in studies were 30 ml of aloe juice per day, or 1000 mg per day. It is not a good idea to start taking aloe vera juice or supplements without consulting your doctor, as it can react with quite a few different medications.

---

2 https://www.healthline.com/nutrition/blood-sugar-supplements#TOC_TITLE_HDR_3, accessed 01.08.2021

5) Berberine

This is a root compound that comes from a few different kinds of plants, and it is thought that taking supplements of it could again reduce your fasting blood sugar level, particularly if combined with changes to your diet, and increased exercise.

It is also thought that berberine could improve the effectiveness of diabetes medication, allowing the dose of medicine to be reduced overall. Berberine may be able to increase the amount of sugar taken in by your muscles, which helps to reduce the amount of sugar in the blood. Taking between 300 and 500 mg with your meals each day is sufficient. Again, berberine can affect other medications and should not be taken without consulting a doctor.

6) Vitamin D

Being deficient in vitamin D could make you more at risk of type 2 diabetes, and taking a supplement of vitamin D is thought to be able to improve both the A1C and the fasting blood sugar levels for a patient. It is thought that Vitamin D could be able to improve the production of insulin in the pancreatic cells, and to boost the way the body responds to insulin.

If you would like to start taking vitamin D supplements, talk to your doctor about what dose would be best for you. They will usually do a blood test so they can prescribe the right level. You should also discuss any medications you are currently taking before you start vitamin D supplements, as they can interact with some types of medicine.

7) Gurmar

The "sugar destroyer" plant, gurmar, may be able to reduce your fasting blood sugar level by nearly 30%. Taking this herb regularly could also reduce your cravings for sweet and sugary foods because it suppresses the taste sensation in your mouth. It may be able to reduce the gut's absorption of sugar, and can increase how much sugar your cells take out of your blood. It has an impact on type 1 diabetes as well as type 2, and it may also be able to increase the amount of insulin produced by the cells in your pancreas.

You can take 200 mg twice a day, preferably with meals. It may increase the effect your blood sugar has on insulin, so if you are taking insulin injections, talk to your doctor before you begin **utilising** this supplement.

8) Magnesium

A surprising number of people with type 2 diabetes have low levels of magnesium in their blood, particularly diabetics who haven't got their blood sugar levels under control. As many as 38% of people with type 2 diabetes may have low levels of magnesium. Magnesium plays a role in the secretion and use of insulin in the tissues of the body.

Several studies have indicated that magnesium supplements can reduce the fasting blood sugar levels in all people, including those without diabetes or prediabetes. You should take magnesium at the same time as eating, and 250-350 mg per day is the recommended dose. You shouldn't take magnesium in conjunction with magnesium oxide. Check with your doctor before starting magnesium supplements, as these can cause problems with other medications, including antibiotics.

9) Alpha-lipoic Acid

Taking alpha-lipoic acid alongside the standard diabetes medication has been shown to improve the fasting blood sugar level and A1C. An increased dose, from 300 mg to 1200 mg, showed improvements, and doses above 600 mg per day should be taken before meals.

Alpha-lipoic acid is an antioxidant produced by the liver. It can also be found in red meat and spinach, as well as certain other foods. It is thought to improve the insulin sensitivity and the uptake of blood sugar by your body's cells. It can take a few months for this to occur. You should not take alpha-lipoic acid if you suffer from hyperthyroid disease. Talk to your doctor before including this in your diet.

10) Chromium

If your body does not have enough chromium, it will struggle to convert carbohydrates into sugars when you need energy, which can increase the amount of insulin required. Supplementing chromium can reduce the A1C of people with type 2 diabetes, and possibly even type 1 diabetes (although further study is needed to confirm this). It is thought that chromium enhances the activity of the pancreatic cells which produce insulin. Alternatively, it may make insulin more effective; it is not currently clear.

The dose has not yet been fixed upon, but many people take 200 mcg each day. However, higher doses of up to 1000 mcg in a day may have a greater effect. Certain medications may reduce your ability to absorb chromium, so speak to a doctor before you begin taking it.

8 Highly Effective Ways To Lower Blood Sugar

When your blood sugar is too high, the fastest and most effective way to deal with it is to take insulin, but in some instances, this may not be an option for you. For the times when you need another solution, we're going to cover some of the best ways to reduce your blood sugar.

If you are having ongoing issues with your blood sugar levels, make sure you couple these strategies with proper management as agreed upon with your doctor.

1) Exercise

Besides medication, exercise is probably the fastest and most effective way to reduce your blood sugar levels. The other great thing about exercise is that it can have a prolonged effect on your blood sugar levels, and may help to keep them low for up to a day after you stop exercising. Essentially, exercise increases your body's sensitivity to insulin, making it more effective at dealing with the sugar in your system. Exercise means that the muscles need energy, and this prompts your body to move glucose to the muscles, which will pull down your blood sugar levels.

However, you should be cautious of brief, high intensity exercises, as these can increase your blood sugar levels temporarily because the body is creating a stress response. Depending on your health, your doctor may suggest checking your blood sugar levels before you partake in any exercise. This is particularly true if you have type 1 diabetes. You should be able to get a urine testing kit to do this at home. These kits check your urine for ketones, and if they are present, they can increase your blood sugar levels to higher than they were before you began exercising.

This is not good for you, so it's important to check your levels before you start exercising, and follow your doctor's advice if they are high. In order for the exercise to have a positive effect on your blood sugar levels, you need to choose an exercise that encourages your heart to pump more quickly. Any exercise will suffice for this, even a brisk walk around the room, or a quick jog. Try exercising to drop your blood sugar levels, even if you just do enough to increase your heart rate mildly. Strenuous exercise is not necessary, and if you do have high ketone levels, could be problematic. However, if your ketone levels are normal, you can do more difficult exercise if you choose to.

2) Balance Your Carbohydrates Carefully

It is a good idea to keep an eye on your carbohydrate intake so that you can maintain a steady level day to day.

Carbohydrates are broken down into sugars by your body, and most of these sugars are glucose. The insulin produced in other parts of the body helps you to process and use or store this sugar. If you eat too many carbohydrates, you put more pressure on the insulin production and use, and make it hard for your body to balance its glucose levels.

Pay attention to carbohydrate recommendations and try to balance your intake of carbohydrates by planning your meals and sticking to a plan. Keeping the number of carbohydrates you consume reasonably low will help to reduce the amount of blood sugar spikes you suffer from, as well as your overall blood sugar levels, both in the short and the long term. If you notice your blood sugar levels climbing, check your intake of carbohydrates and try to reduce them if they are not well balanced.

3) Manage Your Portions

This is easier said than done, but keeping an eye on how much you eat, as well as what you eat, is a good way to balance your blood sugar levels. As mentioned earlier, there is a strong link between obesity and diabetes.

You can benefit from weight reduction even if you only lose a small amount of weight. You don't have to get down to your ideal weight; every decrease in your weight will benefit your health and reduce your chances of developing diabetes.

Portion control plays a big role in this. You should slowly work towards reducing how much you eat at every meal, and aim to fill up on fruits and vegetables when you need a snack. Combine reduced food intake with good exercise in order to lose weight and keep it off. You may find that it helps to set small, achievable goals that you can keep working towards. Don't focus on how much you would like to lose in the long run, but on how much you can realistically lose in a few months.

Getting yourself to a healthy weight is one of the best ways to manage the risk of diabetes, prediabetes, and type 2 diabetes. Don't discount the importance of this.

4) Prioritise Hydration

Being well hydrated can help your kidneys to function well, and they will in turn flush sugar out of your body through your urine, at least to some degree. This can keep the level of sugar in your blood lower.

Try to drink throughout the day, keeping a bottle of water to hand. If you struggle to drink regularly, set an alarm to remind yourself to take regular water breaks. This may reduce your risk of diabetes, or help you to manage diabetes if you already suffer from it.

It is best to just drink water if possible. Any drinks that contain sugar will have a negative impact that will raise your blood sugar levels and should be avoided, especially if you are already having problems. If you find water unappealing, try adding a dash of lemon or a sprig of mint to **flavour** it and give it more appeal. Many people also find cold water easier to enjoy, so make some ice and use it to chill your drinks.

5) Minimise Your Stress

This is often easier said than done, but try to avoid stress if you are struggling with your blood sugar levels; being stressed can raise them. It is best to keep away from or exit stressful situations where possible, because while you are stressed, your body will release certain hormones to try and deal with the stress, and these can cause an increase in the amount of sugar in your blood.

It can be hard to avoid stressful situations sometimes, and being aware that stress is bad for your health can make them even worse. You should try to **minimise** stress by setting certain boundaries, and by learning stress management techniques. Meditation can be a good way of managing stress, and exercise has also been shown to decrease stress levels – as well as helping to regulate your blood sugar levels.

6) Improve Your Sleep

Again, it can be a challenge to manage your sleep levels, but if you can sleep regular hours and get enough sleep on a regular basis, you are more likely to be able to regulate your blood sugar levels properly. Lack of sleep can make it hard for your body to know what to do with excess sugars, and you may find that your blood sugar levels are significantly higher if you do not sleep well – whereas when you are rested, they should be lower. Try to set a regular sleep schedule and stick to it. Proper rest is key to many other aspects of your health, so taking the time to sleep well and **prioritising** healthy sleep habits is good for more than just the regulation of your blood sugar levels.

7) Include Apple Cider Vinegar In Your Diet

Vinegar is an important means of improving your insulin sensitivity, although you should check in with your doctor before you start to consume it in quantities, especially if you are on medication to lower your blood sugar level – or you could drop your blood sugar level dangerously. Using vinegar regularly can decrease your fasting blood sugar level. You can either include it in your diet, or mix some with water and drink it before consuming a meal that is high in carbohydrates. Many people enjoy it as an alternative to other vinegars as it has a very pleasant **flavour**.

8) Eat Plenty Of Fibre

Eating a high **fibre** diet is a good way to reduce your blood sugar levels. Both soluble and insoluble **fibre** are important to reducing your blood sugar levels because they decrease the speed with which sugar and carbohydrates are absorbed into the blood, and make your blood sugar levels rise more slowly.

Soluble **fibre** is particularly useful when it comes to managing your blood sugar, but any **fibre** in your diet is useful for reducing sugar lows or spikes. Try to include lots of lean proteins, whole grains, and plenty of vegetables. Men should be trying to consume around 38 grams of **fibre** per day, while women only need around 25 grams. Some of the above strategies take longer to work than others, but all will help to regulate your blood sugar levels, and some have both short-term and long-term effects. Combine the strategies given here to **maximise** their effectiveness and regulate your blood sugar levels as best you can. It is always a good idea to discuss the steps you are taking at home with your health practitioner as well. This will ensure that your doctor is able to take them into account when **organising** your care plan, and offer advice on your approach.

Why Is A Diabetic Diet So Effective With Weight Loss?

We have mentioned weight loss as an important aspect of managing diabetes, and it is certain that dieting and reducing your weight is key to both reducing your risk of diabetes and keeping on top of the disease if you develop it.

It may surprise you to learn that you don't even need to lose significant amounts of weight in order to improve your insulin sensitivity and get in control of your blood sugar levels. A study[3] showed that losing just 7% of your weight could improve your insulin sensitivity by more than 50%, which makes a massive difference to your ability to manage your blood sugar levels. This is a goal that many people will find achievable, and it can make an extraordinary difference to your health.

An appropriate diet for people suffering from diabetes involves balancing protein, fats, and carbohydrates, with key emphasis on reducing the consumption of carbohydrates to ideal levels. Most people who suffer from diabetes should be getting 45% or less of their daily calories from the carbohydrates they consume (although bear in mind that you should check this with your doctor; this depends on your specific circumstances, how much exercise you do, and any medication that you may be taking).

It is important also to choose carbohydrates that don't cause a spike in your blood sugar levels. That means high-**fibre** foods such as whole grains, vegetables like carrots, squashes, cabbages, and salad greens, and oily fish. You should avoid things like dried fruit, sugary yogurt, sugary cereals, white bread, white pasta, white rice, maple syrup, and honey. These foods are high in sugar and your intake of them should be limited.

You should also aim to focus on protein but keep your calories low. Protein is important for keeping your muscles strong, which will help you to keep burning calories and keep your weight down. Look for lean protein sources such as fish and tofu.

Unsaturated fats are another important aspect of the diet, and you can get these from fish, avocados, nuts, olive oil, etc. Try to avoid fatty fried foods and meat.

This diet, paired with exercise, will quickly aid weight loss because it helps you to reduce your sugar intake significantly, and also aims to balance the number of calories that come from carbohydrates, which can cause quick weight gain. Note that you do not have to completely stick to the suggestions above, but that implementing them anywhere you can will help you to reduce your weight and feel better.

3Diabetes Care. Author manuscript; available in PMC 2005 Nov 10.

Published in final edited form as:

Diabetes Care. 2002 Dec; 25(12): 2165–2171.

doi: 10.2337/diacare.25.12.2165

5 Scientifically Proven Ways To Accelerate Sustainable And Healthy Weight Loss

When it comes to losing weight, it is crucial to approach the process safely, preferably with the help of a medical professional, especially if you have struggled with weight issues for some time. Remember that in order for weight loss to be effective, it must be sustainable – and that usually means losing weight fairly slowly, perhaps at a couple of pounds per week.

It is not unusual to find yourself feeling hungry if you attempt to start dieting, but with a careful approach, you should be able to avoid this issue. Finding places where you can cut out sugar and using fresh vegetables to fill in when you need a snack are good starting points, but let's look at some of the other ways in which you can safely and sustainably lose weight.

1) Take A Cold Shower

Taking a cold shower is a great way to burn off brown fat. These are cells that generate heat by burning off the fat that they contain, so taking a cold shower is a great way to stimulate them to do this – and this can help you lose the fat they contain.

These cells tend to be in the upper part of the body, particularly around your shoulders and your neck – which is where water from the shower will usually hit. A cold shower is therefore a perfect way to deal with these fat cells and reduce them.

2) L-Glutamine

Glutamine is a naturally occurring amino acid. It can be bought as a supplement, or got from certain foods such as meat, eggs, and whey.

Further research is needed to help understand the link between glutamine supplements and weight-loss. Several studies have been done in which people taking L-Glutamine supplements reduced fat and belly fat, and decreased their waist circumference in just a few weeks. This included a study done on those with type 2 diabetes, which also found a reduced risk of heart disease.

However, thus far, the studies have been done in the short term and on very small sample sizes. If you wish to look into taking glutamine as a supplement to help with weight loss, discuss the implications with your doctor and see whether they believe you could benefit from the supplement. At present, research is too limited to say for sure whether it will help with weight loss.

3) Berberine

We mentioned berberine as a valuable supplement earlier, but it's worth reiterating its usefulness here. A plant alkaloid, berberine is often used to reduce insulin resistance and fight the effects of type 2 diabetes. It helps to increase insulin sensitivity by inhibiting Protein-Tyrosine Phosphatase 1B, and activating Adenosine Monophosphate-Activated Protein Kinase.

It is also thought that it may be able to reduce the triglycerides and LDL-cholesterol in type 2 diabetes.

Berberine may be as effective for treating type 2 diabetes as metformin or glibenclamide (when taken in 1500 mg quantities, substituted for an equal amount of the appropriate medication). However, while quite a few studies indicate that this is the case, further research is needed before it can be used as a substitute for the medication; it has not been as thoroughly studied as existing prescribed medicines. The long-term effects are, as yet, unclear.

4) Eat More Slowly

Eating slowly is a great technique for losing weight; quick eating often leads to weight gain. Eating slowly helps you to feel full faster, and so you will be satisfied with smaller portions, while if you eat fast, you are much more likely to decide you need a second helping.

Chewing slowly can reduce the calories that you consume during a meal, and it is also thought that eating slowly can produce a weight-reducing hormone, so as well as eating less overall, you will be more actively losing weight. If you are struggling to implement this technique, try using a timer for your meals and set a certain amount of minutes for each one. You will also find that you enjoy your food more overall, and this will probably make it easier to stick to a diet.

5) Have Plenty Of Protein At Breakfast

Eating a lot of protein early in the day will help you to feel full for much longer. Choose something like a boiled egg with whole grain bread to accompany it. This will reduce your cravings and your overall calorie intake each day.

Set yourself up for a great day by starting with high-protein options; this will put you in a good position to achieve your eating goals for the rest of the day. It is worth taking the time to have a great, healthy breakfast, rather than rushing through and eating a junk, high-sugar food that will soon leave you feeling hungry and craving something sweet to fill the gap.

If you don't eat eggs, choose another high-protein food and attempt to include some grain options too. This combination is the best breakfast for keeping your weight down.

Remember, sustained weight loss is about losing weight slowly and making consistently healthy choices while still allowing yourself the occasional treat. You do not have to give up all the things you enjoy. Just try to cut back on the quantities that you eat, and make sensible choices that will help you to feel full without the sugar hits that many people turn to.

7 Common Mistakes In Diabetes Management And How To Avoid Them

So, we've discussed some of the things that you should do to best manage your diabetes – what about the things that you should not do? How can you avoid making diabetes worse or triggering blood sugar spikes or lows?

1) Not Eating Regularly

Your sugar levels will spike when you eat, and drop when you don't eat for a while, so eating irregular meals is a sure way to make your sugar levels fluctuate sharply. You should not go for hours on end without eating; try to plan your meals so that you are eating regularly throughout the day, and you don't ever leave a significant period between your meals.

It is a good idea to eat small meals on a regular plan, rather than eating big meals. A large serving will make you feel full for longer, even once your blood sugar levels have started to drop, and you'll also find it more difficult to manage your weight if you eat big, frequent meals. Instead, try to go for a small serving every few hours.

You can also use snacks to keep your sugar levels steady, but avoid high-sugar options. For example, it's best to choose vegetables over high-sugar fruits. If you do want to eat fruit, opt for options that contain plenty of **fibre** to help your body deal with the sugar. Raspberries, pears, and unpeeled apples are excellent choices.

If you are regularly out and about, consider carrying some small snacks with you at all times so that you have something to eat if you get delayed and can't eat according to your meal plan. This can help you avoid having a sugar crash, tiding you over until you can eat a proper meal.

2) Avoiding All Carbohydrates

Some people assume that because carbohydrates can cause issues with your blood sugar levels, you should avoid them as much as you can, but this is not the case. You need carbohydrates, and diets that reduce them too much can be very unhealthy. You won't get proper nutrition from a diet that is very low in carbohydrates, so don't just take the "reduce your carbs" rule as a hard and fast rule to be followed in every instance.

Instead, take a look at the glycemic index, which tells you the glycemic loads in different foods. You can find out which carbohydrates will keep your blood sugar levels steady, and which will cause them to spike. Complex carbohydrates, often found in things like brown rice and whole grain breads, are generally good, while simple carbohydrates, found in corn syrup, brown sugar, and white bread, are bad.

Plan your meals to include complex carbohydrates instead of simple ones, and make sure you are aware when you are consuming simple carbohydrates so you can keep an eye on your blood sugar levels.

3) Avoid Full Cheat Days

People talk about "banking" carbohydrates. This is when you avoid eating carbohydrate-heavy foods for six days of the week, and then enjoy a cheat day where you can eat whatever you want. However, this is not a good idea for people who suffer from diabetes. Having a whole day of eating "treat" foods and sugary snacks will play havoc with your blood sugar levels and will not make you feel good at all. It also won't help you stay on track with your weight loss goals and may cause you to crave these foods more strongly during other days of the week. Cheat days are not a good way to handle diabetes. However, it is okay to have treats from time to time, and doing so can actually make it easier to stay on track with your diet. You can "bank" carbohydrates on a much smaller scale. Rather than saving up for the whole week, try saving up for just one day if you know you want to eat something that's heavy in simple carbohydrates at dinner. This can be a great way to reward yourself in a controlled manner, and should have minimal impact on your diet.

Use this method sparingly and be sensible about your "treat" intake. If you eat birthday cake every day, you're going to struggle to stay on track with your diet, even if you try banking these carbohydrates from other meals.

4) Depending Too Much Or Too Little On Medication

Medication is a crucial part of managing your diabetes, but it is not everything. You need to balance using medication with good health practices, making sure you exercise and eat well, rather than just trusting the prescribed medicine to deal with your health issues.

It is crucial that you keep your doctor up to date about your health and fitness. You should keep logs about your blood sugar levels, the steps you are taking to keep them steady, and the symptoms you're experiencing. These logs can be shared with your doctor on a regular basis and they can then adjust the treatment they provide from an informed position. Do not decide to cut your doctor out of your health decisions; talk to them when you make changes, discuss things that you want to try, and generally keep them informed about everything you are doing.

This is particularly important if you are taking supplements or using other remedies that you think may be able to help. It is okay to try things, but keep your doctor updated so they can alter their approach to your diabetes when necessary.

On the other hand, do not depend too heavily on your doctor and the medicine they provide. Medication is not the sole solution to diabetes, and it needs to be combined with good management in order to work well. You can't just eat anything you fancy and then take your medicine and assume it will be fine. You need to adjust your lifestyle to account for and manage your diabetes, or you will find that your medication is not as effective as it should be.

Discuss a health plan with your doctor, and let them know if you are struggling to stick to it. They may be able to make alterations or find methods to get you back on track. Medicine and your health practitioner need to be treated as part of the solution – neither ignored, nor depended upon too heavily. You will get the best results if you include your doctor in your decisions but make efforts to manage your diabetes yourself.

5) Not Eating Enough Protein

We discussed the importance of protein for keeping your muscles strong earlier. Protein will help to slow down the use of carbohydrates, making them convert into sugars more gradually. Including protein whenever you eat carbohydrates is key to keeping your blood sugar levels stable, so find some easy-to-eat, high protein foods that you enjoy, and include them with every meal, especially meals that are high in sugar.

Some good snacks include adding peanut butter to apple slices, or eating things like hard boiled eggs, jerky, nuts, cottage cheese, and pumpkin seeds. Having a handful of seeds alongside a carbohydrate-based snack will help to reduce the sugar spike and make it easier for you to keep your blood sugar levels stable. If you're going to eat a chocolate bar, try to have a few nuts alongside it.

6) Deciding You Are Cured

If you're doing really well at managing your diabetes, your blood sugar levels might be consistently normal month after month. With a few positive A1C tests, you might feel that you've done everything you need to do and your diabetes has gone away, so you can eat whatever you want to going forward.

Unfortunately, this is not the case. Type 2 diabetes can go into remission or even be reversed, but you will not ever fully cure it, and you should not assume that you can start eating unhealthy foods just because you have done well recently. Even if you manage to reverse your type 2 diabetes, you need to eat sensibly and exercise properly going forward to ensure you remain healthy. Keep an eye on your blood sugar levels and think about the foods you are consuming at all times.

7) Not Exercising Properly

It's easy to think about exercising and much harder to do it. You may have an exercise plan written down, but be struggling to follow it because things just keep getting in the way. Unfortunately, it can be a challenge to consistently exercise, but this is one of the biggest mistakes you can make when it comes to managing your diabetes properly.

You need to exercise in order to reduce your blood sugar levels and increase your circulation. Your blood vessels will suffer when your blood sugar levels are high, and working out can improve their health and make sure your blood is flowing properly. Using your muscles will burn up excess sugars in your blood and make sure you are using carbohydrates up rather than allowing them to turn into fat.

Exercising regularly is key to managing your weight. Coupled with healthy eating, it can help to control diabetes. It is not the only aspect of good management, but it is crucial, especially if you are struggling with your weight and healthy eating. Don't dismiss the importance of exercise.

If you are failing to find a kind of exercise that suits you, talk to your doctor about your options. There are so many exercises you can do, and different things work for different people. For example, you may find that working out a gym is what motivates you, or you might prefer to exercise from the comfort of your own home. Find ways to reward yourself and keep yourself motivated so that fitness is a part of your routine

3 Powerful Health Apps For Diabetes

Utilising the power of technology is a great way to manage your diabetes, and many apps have been developed that can help you get on top of your condition and continue to enjoy a healthy life while keeping your blood sugar levels normal. Apps have been shown to be effective both for managing weight loss and for handling type 2 diabetes, so they're another tool in your arsenal in the fight against diabetes.

That said, there are a lot of options out there and only so much time in which to try them all out. Instead of clogging up your phone with forty different apps and then getting overwhelmed and never using any of them, you need to know which are likely to work for you. Of course, everyone is different and what you find effective, another might find useless, but this should at least give you a starting point for choosing the right app for you. We'll cover three of the best options so you can try them out and see what you think.

1) Fooducate

Fooducate is top of our list, and as the name suggests, it's about educating you on what's in your food. Knowledge is power, as they say, and knowing what your food contains will give you more power to handle your diabetes properly.

Fooducate allows you to search for or scan different foods and grades the quality of the calories contained within that food. This will help you work out which foods you can eat to keep your blood sugar levels steady, and makes it much easier for you to detect when a food is not good for you. For example, it can help you identify foods that have hidden sugars or ingredients you might not expect.

Essentially, Fooducate is about empowering you to eat better food and avoid foods that aren't good for you personally. You can use the app for free (with some in-app purchases) and find out more about what you're consuming before you put it in your mouth.

2) Medical ID

This might sound like a bad idea aiming to replace doctors, but it isn't at all – and in fact, it's a great app for anyone, not just those who suffer from diabetes. It allows you to create a medical profile that gives first responders information about who you are and how to treat you if an emergency should arise. This is key if you have any allergies or take any medication, and it could show someone how to help you if you suffer from a severe sugar crash or spike.

The app's information can be accessed even when the phone is locked, meaning that people can help you whether you are conscious or not. You can also add emergency contact information so they know who to get in touch with to help you. While this app isn't specifically geared for helping with diabetes, it could save your life in an emergency, and it's totally free to use.

If you were to have a **hypoglycaemic** event and find yourself incapable of speech, this app could be enough to help those around you know how to assist.

3) Glucose Buddy

This app allows users to track their insulin, medication, blood glucose levels, carbohydrate intake, and A1C results. It is essentially an all-in-one guide for diabetic care and will monitor your health in both the long and short term.

It can be synced with monitoring systems such as the Dexcom G5 and G6 to keep records of your blood sugar levels over time. The chart display it offers will allow you to view trends and get a better understanding of how your blood sugar levels work. These can be shared with your doctor to improve your treatment and ensure that your medication is helping you properly.

It also has options for tracking the exercise you do and the food that you eat, making it easier for you to stay on target with food and fitness plans. If you're struggling to stay on track, this could be particularly handy. The app even provides notifications reminding you to check your blood sugar levels, decreasing your chances of missing a check.

The app is free, but also has subscription services that can further improve your diabetes. These include things like an A1C calculator, coaching for diabetes, reports on performance, and glucose meters. The free experience does include ads, while the subscription services are ad-free. They can cost up to $59.99 per month, although there are cheaper options at $19.99. You may find that you benefit from these extra services, or you might prefer to use the free one.

Approved Food List For Diabetes

You may find that it helps you to have an approved list of foods you can turn to. Diabetes is a complex disease to handle, so having some go-to foods is important, especially early on in your diagnosis, when it may seem overwhelming to try and deal with all the information that you have to take on board. Here are some foods that you can turn to when you are struggling to manage your diabetes. Remember to balance your portion sizes, combine proteins with carbohydrates, and focus on vegetables, high-**fibre** fruits, and whole grains as much as possible.

- Fatty fish, such as salmon, mackerel, herring, and anchovies. These protect your blood vessels from inflammation and provide plenty of protein that can regulate your blood sugar levels.
- Leafy greens, such as kale and spinach.
- Beans, which are rich in vitamins and nutrients like potassium, magnesium, and **fibre**.
- Eggs, which increase your good cholesterol and improve your insulin sensitivity.
- Greek yogurt (with no added sugar), which may be able to reduce insulin resistance and lower the glucose in your blood.
- Extra virgin olive oil, which can improve glycemic management and has antioxidant properties. It can also lower your triglyceride levels after a meal, and many diabetics have high triglyceride levels.
- Apple cider vinegar, which can reduce blood sugar by up to 20% when consumed with meals with carbohydrates.
- Strawberries: although many fruits are not suitable for diabetics because of the high sugar content, strawberries have an antioxidant called anthocyanin in them. They can enhance your insulin sensitivity and improve blood sugar levels.
- Garlic, which is highly nutritious and can help to reduce your blood pressure and improve your blood's glucose management.
- Squashes, both summer (e.g. **courgettes**) and winter varieties (e.g. pumpkins and butternut squash). These are low sugar and low calorie, and contain antioxidants. Pumpkin contains polysaccharides, which decreased the levels of serum glucose when tested on animals.
- Flaxseed/linseed, which has insoluble **fibre**, omega-3 fats, and can lower your blood pressure.
-

Try to avoid:

- High salt foods
- Red meats
- Processed meats
- Lard
- Butter
- Added sugar (so try to reduce the amount that you take in tea, coffee, etc., over a period of time)
- Alcohol, which has a lot of calories in

How To Manage Type 2 Diabetes And Nutritional Adjustments

You will note that there is a great deal of overlap between managing diabetes and type 2 diabetes. This is essentially because diabetes leads to type 2 diabetes, and therefore the same treatments and prevention methods are used for them. However, bear in mind that if you have type 2 diabetes, it is already more serious and needs more careful management than if you have diabetes. That is not to say that diabetes should be ignored, but if you have type 2 diabetes, mismanagement could swiftly lead to unpleasant consequences. You have less time to get on top of the condition than if you are suffering from diabetes. With that in mind, let's look at the steps you can take to get in control of type 2 diabetes.

Exercise: Again, exercise is a key weapon in your arsenal against type 2 diabetes. You should set an exercise routine and stick to it every week. While it's healthy to have rest days, these need to be part of the overall plan and on the whole, you shouldn't miss your exercise routine in normal circumstances. It may take a while to build up to a healthy exercise regime, so don't rush into this. Talk to your doctor about how you can start getting fit. If you are very overweight, find exercises that won't put excessive stress on your joints. Running is not a great choice if you are carrying a lot of extra pounds. You may find that swimming is a better option, since it allows you to burn off calories and exercise a lot of your muscles, and doesn't put much stress on your body. You can mix this with other kinds of exercise. If you can find something fun to do, such as a team sport you enjoy, you are much more likely to find that you keep exercising than if you just try and slog it out with something that you hate. Choose a few different kinds of exercise and try as many of them as you can to maximise the benefit you get.

Medication: If you have got type 2 diabetes, you will probably be prescribed medication to help you deal with it alongside your lifestyle changes. This dose may change as your diabetes changes, so it's important to keep reviewing it with your doctor on a regular basis. Usually, doctors start patients on metformin first. This will be given to you for a trial period, after which the doctor may decide to change it for another medication if it is not having the desired result. In later years, your doctor may prescribe insulin, but this is not usually a first-resort with type 2 diabetes as it is better to manage it with other medication first. Insulin is usually given when other medications are proving ineffective.

You may experience side effects as a result of your medication, but you should continue to take it. These could include:

- Nausea
- Weight gain
- Weight loss
- Bloating
- Diarrhoea

Talk to your doctor if you are experiencing side effects, but don't stop taking your medication unless you are told that you can.

Blood Sugar Management: Managing your blood sugar becomes even more important with type 2 diabetes. You may be given a management plan by your doctor, along with a method for measuring your blood sugar. It is important that you do regular checks.

You will probably also be invited for a regular A1C test every three months so that your doctor can check your blood sugar levels are within a suitable range and make any necessary adjustments to your medication. Follow your doctor's guidance about any other checks you need to do.

Nutritional Adjustments: Healthy eating also becomes more crucial with type 2 diabetes. You need to be stricter about cutting out simple carbohydrates and sugary foods. Remove snacks like dried fruit from your diet entirely if possible. Stop drinking fruit juice, cut back on alcohol, and make sure that any sugar you eat is paired with protein. You should also eat less fresh fruit unless it is fibrous.

Remember that if you want to eat something sugary, you can "bank" carbohydrates for a day, but you should not eat a lot of sugar even then. It is important to keep your blood sugar levels as normal as you can, and not allow them to spike by eating something sweet just because you have been "good" all day.

Choose easy snacks that you can turn to when you aren't able to eat a meal. This will keep your blood sugar levels steady. Nuts, peanut butter, crackers, and whole grain bread are good options for this. It is a good idea to carry snacks if you are going to be out for long, as not eating for long periods can cause sugar crashes.

Nutrition will become key to keeping your blood sugars normal and ensuring that you keep the condition under control as much as possible. Talk to your doctor about the best way to plan your diet, and keep a meal plan that specifically focuses on cutting out the sugar and simple carbohydrates.

Give Up Smoking If You Smoke: As mentioned, giving up smoking can raise your blood sugar levels for some time, so it is best to discuss this with your doctor. Although they will likely still advise that you give up smoking, they may prefer you to wait until your blood sugar levels have **normalised** before you do so. It's best to take medical direction on this, rather than depending on other sources.

How To Manage Type 1 Diabetes and Nutritional Adjustments

Treating type 1 diabetes can be more complicated than type 2, and you should again defer to guidance from your doctor about this condition. However, here are some general rules that may help you to stay in control of type 1 diabetes.

Exercise: Exercise is still an important aspect of managing type 1 diabetes, but it needs to be approached more carefully because exercising can cause sugar highs (**hyperglycaemia**) and sugar lows (**hypoglycaemia**). You usually need to check your blood glucose level before you start exercising and during exercise in order to make sure you are safe to keep exercising. A blood check will let you know if (and what) you need to eat, and when your insulin needs adjusting. Bear in mind that there are different kinds of exercise and they will affect your body in different ways. For example, moderate but lasting exercise, such as walking, will cause your blood glucose levels to slowly drop. Fast, short bursts of exercise can cause them to rise. Eating the right amount of carbohydrates for the kind of exercise you are doing and your current blood sugar level is important.

You will probably need to spend time working out an exercise routine with your doctor, and it may take some trial and error to get it right. However, exercise is a good way to manage your diabetes and can help reduce the glucose spikes that occur from eating.

It's a good idea to keep checking your blood glucose levels even when you have stopped exercising, as exercise can have an effect for twelve hours after you finish. Make sure you eat something or take a dose of insulin before you go to sleep if necessary.

Staying hydrated while you exercise is also important.

Medication: If you have type 1 diabetes, you will be taking insulin. This is often coupled with other management techniques, including exercise, a good diet, regular blood sugar level checks, and balanced fats, proteins, and carbohydrates.

There are several different kinds of insulin, which include:

- Short-acting insulin
- Rapid-acting insulin
- Intermediate-acting insulin
- Long-acting insulin

Your doctor will help you understand these and when they should be used.

Blood Sugar Management: You will be regularly checking your blood sugar levels if you suffer from type 1 diabetes. You will usually check your levels before you eat something, before, during, and after exercise, and before you go to sleep. You may also need to check during the night and at other times.

These levels will be discussed with your doctor and used to hone your treatment.

Nutritional Adjustments: Although type 1 diabetes is not caused by unhealthy eating, it is still important to treat it by avoiding sugars and simple carbohydrates, as these will affect blood sugar levels just as they will with type 2 diabetes and prediabetes.

You will need to manage your diet by keeping unhealthy fats low, avoiding sugars, and making sure that you consume enough **fibre**. Fruits, vegetables, beans, and whole grains are still the best options for someone with type 1 diabetes.

In order to manage the condition well, you will need to focus heavily on your diet and learn to read your insulin levels so that you know what to eat. Often, you will find that it is a fine balance. Your doctor should guide you on how to approach your meals so that you get the best possible results from your food intake and keep your blood sugar levels as steady as possible.

Often, you will need to specifically count your carbohydrates and the amount of fat and protein that you consume.

Give Up Smoking If You Smoke: Giving up smoking can help you manage type 1 diabetes, but it is again something that you should discuss with your doctor before attempting. It will improve your overall health and your circulation, and make it easier to exercise well.

Many people who suffer from type 1 diabetes find it hard to give up smoking, but with support from your doctor and other professionals, it is possible, and doing so will majorly improve your health.

Lifestyle Changes To Improve And Manage Diabetes Successfully

For the final section, we'll discuss some of the ways you can improve your lifestyle to make your diabetes management easier and more effective. Remember that everyone is different, and you should discuss major changes with your doctor before implementing them so that your specific circumstances and any other medication that you take can be accounted for.

Set Personal <u>Behavioural</u> Goals & Form Strong Habits For A Healthier Life

Part of managing diabetes effectively means forming habits that will last. You need to make a long-term commitment to dealing with the condition and staying on top of it. Short-term, well-intentioned bursts of healthy eating are not sufficient to manage the disease, so you need to take a truly proactive and dedicated approach to it, and ensure that you stay on the right track. You should talk to others who suffer from the disease, as well as your doctor and your loved ones, in order to identify goals that will work for you. There is no point in setting unachievable goals that you can't meet, because you will only frustrate yourself and make it harder and more unpleasant to manage the condition. Instead, choose some exercise, weight loss, and eating goals that are realistic for where you currently are, and then consider long-term goals that will help you as you move forward. Remember, as mentioned earlier, you do not need to lose a lot of weight to dramatically increase your insulin sensitivity. Losing less than 10% of your body weight increases your insulin sensitivity by over 50%. Set your weight loss goals with your doctor, discussing what is realistic. It is important not to over-exercise and then lose your motivation; in the fight against diabetes, slow and steady, habit-forming exercise is more important than an enthusiastic but swift burnout.

Fundamentals Of A Diabetic Diet For Over 50s

If you are over 50, you might find it harder to manage your diet when diagnosed with diabetes. There are two major problems you may experience: difficulty losing weight, and **hypoglycaemia**. Difficulty losing weight: this occurs because as you get older, your cells will increase their resistance to insulin, and it will become harder for you to process sugars. This often leads to people gaining belly fat. You are also likely to observe your metabolism slowing down, at least a bit, as you get older. You will need to further reduce your intake of refined carbohydrates and increase the number of vegetables that you eat. Whole grains will also become more important. You will probably need to keep a food diary to chart what you eat during the week, and stick to a fitness regime as prescribed by your doctor. Losing weight is not impossible as you age, but it is much harder, so bear this in mind and try not to be too disappointed by your results.

Hypoglycaemia: you are also more vulnerable to **hypoglycaemia** as you age, particularly if you take diabetes medication. Your kidneys stop functioning as effectively, and this means that your diabetes medication may remain in your body for longer than it is supposed to. This can result in a drop in your blood sugar level, especially if you are on other kinds of medications or you regularly skip meals.

If you suffer from **hypoglycaemia**, you may notice tingling in your mouth, blurry vision, confusion, or dizziness. If you do experience **hypoglycaemia**, even once, you should discuss this with your doctor as your medication may need adjusting.

What Is A Normal Blood Sugar Level For People At Age 50?

If you do not have diabetes, your blood sugar level should be below 150 mg / dL when you have passed 50. At younger than 50, your blood sugar levels should be less than 140 mg / dL, so there is not a big difference based on age. This is following a meal.

After fasting, a blood sugar level for a 50 year old should be around 100 mg / dL.

Adjustments For Diabetic Diet For People over 50

If you are over 50, you may be wondering how to adjust your diet to account for diabetes. It is important for you to try and keep your weight down and your blood sugar levels as stable as possible. This will account for your difficulty in losing weight and the challenges presented by low blood sugar.

Regular snacks that are low in carbohydrates and high in protein are a good start. Try to take a break and eat a healthy snack every few hours so that your blood sugar levels stay stable. You may find that snacks such as carrots are ideal; they will provide some energy but not cause a spike in your blood sugar.

Focus on fresh vegetables in particular, as these will give you plenty of nutrition without causing weight gain. If you are concerned about handling your diet as an over-50 diabetic, talk to your doctor about the most important nutrients you should include.

The 21 Day Diabetes Action Plan

With this meal plan, you will begin nourishing your body from the inside out. Get yourself on the right track by planning and preparing as much as you can. Remember that this is not about counting calories; it is about getting the right balance of nutrients for your body: vegetables, healthy fats, energizing proteins, and complex carbohydrates high in fibre. The plan includes a snack after every meal. I recommend eating snacks about two to three hours after your main meals in my diabetes management program. If you are hungry less than 2 hours after eating, you should examine whether you are eating balanced, satisfying meals. If it has been between 2 and 3 hours since your last meal, choose low-carb snacks: non starchy veggies, proteins, and healthy fats. If it has been more than 3 to 4 hours since you last ate, include at least one serving of carbs (15 grams of carbs) along with a veggie, protein, and/or healthy fat. Snacking after dinner can be beneficial if eaten at least an hour or more before you go to bed. It is recommended that you do not fast for longer than 10 hours. A bedtime snack that contains about 20 grams of carbs, combined with a protein, prevents the liver from releasing stored glucose into the bloodstream the next morning.

Foods You Need In Your Pantry Every Week

To prepare for the recipes ahead, here is a list of pantry staples that will be helpful.

- Almond butter
- Almonds, unsalted
- Anchovy paste
- Baking powder
- Barley, pearl
- Basil, dried
- Bay leaves
- Breadcrumbs, gluten free
- Cashews
- Chia seeds
- Chili powder, chipotle
- Cherries, dried
- Cinnamon, ground
- Cloves, ground
- Cocoa powder, unsweetened
- Coconut flakes, unsweetened
- Coriander, ground
- Corn-starch
- Cumin, ground
- Curry powder
- Fennel seeds, ground
- Flaxseed, ground
- Flour, whole-wheat
- Garlic powder
- Ginger, ground
- Hemp seeds
- Honey
- Italian seasoning blend, dried
- Lentils, brown
- Honey, pure
- Non-stick cooking spray (olive, coconut, or canola oil)
- Oats, quick
- Oats, rolled
- Oil, canola
- Oil, coconut
- Oil, olive
- Oil, sesame
- Onion, dried, minced
- Onion powder
- Oregano, dried
- Paprika, ground
- Peanut butter, unsalted, natural
- Peanuts, unsalted
- Pepitas (shelled, toasted pumpkin seeds)
- Pepper, cayenne, ground
- Pepper, red, crushed or flakes
- Peppercorns, black
- Peppercorns, white
- Quinoa
- Raisins, unsweetened
- Rice, brown
- Sage, dried, ground
- Salt
- Soy sauce, low sodium, gluten free
- Tahini
- Thyme, dried
- Walnuts
- Worcestershire sauce
- Vanilla extract, pure
- Vinegar, apple cider

Foods You Need In Your Refrigerator Every Week

Maintaining a clean and well-stocked refrigerator will benefit you more than you may think. Clutter-free kitchens promote better outcomes for you, as well as reducing food waste. To ensure you always have the building blocks for an easy, diabetes-friendly meal, start with these staples.

- Eggs
- Favourite veggies, washed and chopped
- Fresh proteins such as fish and poultry (stored in the bottom drawer to prevent potential cross-contamination)
- Homemade salad dressings (perfect for marinades or quick salads)
- Hummus, guacamole, salsa, or another favourite dip
- Low-carb milk alternatives (unsweetened almond, coconut, or cashew)
- Low-sodium tamari, soy sauce, or coconut aminos (adds flavour without adding carbs)
- Mustard, whole-grain, and Dijon (great for dressings)
- Plain yogurt (Greek yogurt is high in protein, but any plain yogurt is an easy add-in)
- Plant-based proteins such as precooked lentils and tofu
- Prewashed leafy greens (you're more likely to eat them when they're accessible and convenient)

Foods You Need In Your Freezer Every Week

I always recommend keeping the following in your freezer:

- Salmon, shrimp, cod, and/or any other favourite seafood
- Dark chocolate (I always keep a dark chocolate bar in my freezer for quick treats)
- Edamame (easy snack high in protein which can be eaten anytime of the day)
- Frozen meat and poultry such as boneless chicken breasts, grass-fed beef, and lean ground turkey
- Frozen mixed berries (great for smoothies)
- Frozen vegetables (I like spinach, broccoli, and green beans)
- Homemade frozen meals, snacks, and one-bite desserts
- Riced cauliflower (a quick and easy low-carb side dish)

Days 1 - 7

Anything new can be challenging on the first day and the first week. As you begin the first few days, I encourage you to be inspired by the results to come.

You will begin days 1 - 7 to retrain your taste buds to crave less sugar and less salt. When you cook more balanced meals at home and eat better quality foods, you will re-sensitize your taste buds and the foods you eat will begin to taste sweeter. The taste buds regenerate approximately every 10 to 12 days, so you will be more than halfway there after your first week!

Check your pantry staples before you head to the grocery store. This shopping list will not repeat them as you will need them every week going forward.

DAY 1 - 7 SHOPPING LIST

FRESH PRODUCE

Apples (2)
Arugula (30 g)
Avocados (3)
Beet (1)
Bell pepper, green (1)
Bell peppers, red (4)
Berries, mixed (950 g)
Blueberries (460 g)
Brussels sprouts (450 g)
Carrots (1 bunch)
Cauliflower (1 head)
Coriander, fresh (1 bunch)
Cucumber (1)
Dill, fresh (1 bunch)
Garlic (2 heads)
Kale (1 bunch)
Lemons (5)
Lettuce, leaf (1 head)
Limes (2)
Microgreens (25 g)
Mint, fresh (1 bunch)
Mushrooms, brown (340 g)
Mushrooms, shiitake (2 or 3)
Onion, red (1)
Onions, yellow (5)
Parsley, fresh (1 bunch)
Peaches (2)
Pepper, jalapeño (1)
Pepper, poblano (1)
Rosemary, fresh (1 bunch)
Scallions (1 bunch)
Spinach (140 g)
Squash, spaghetti (1)
Thyme, fresh (1 bunch)
Tomato, Roma (1)
Tomatoes, cherry (460 g)
Vegetables for roasting such as broccoli, asparagus, bell peppers, onions, cauliflower (950 g)
Vegetables for snacking such as cauliflower, radishes, cucumbers, bell peppers (1.2 kg)
Zucchini, small (8)

DAIRY AND EGGS

Cheese, cheddar, shredded (85 g)
Cheese, mozzarella, shredded (25 g)
Cheese, string (5 pieces)
Cottage cheese, low-fat (460 g)
Eggs (18)
Goat cheese, crumbled (140 g)
Greek yogurt, plain, non-fat (950 g plus 170 g)
Yogurt, unsweetened, vanilla, non-fat (170 g)

CANNED AND BOTTLED ITEMS

Almond milk, unsweetened, plain (4 ¾ dl)
Applesauce, unsweetened (230 g)
Artichoke hearts (1 [400-g] can)
Black beans, low-sodium (2 [430-g] cans)
Coconut milk, unsweetened, plain (4 ¾ dl)
Chicken broth, low sodium (9 ½ dl)
Enchilada sauce (1 [280-g] can)
Sun-dried tomatoes (14 g)
Thai red curry paste (1 [110-g] jar)
Tomatoes, whole (1 [790-g] can)
Vegetable broth, low sodium (9 ½ dl)

FROZEN FOODS

Cauliflower (450 g)

MEAT AND FISH

Canadian bacon (55 g)
Chicken breasts, boneless, skinless (2)
Chicken legs (6)
Salmon fillet (450 g)

Shrimp (230 g)
Trout, whole, cleaned, deboned (2)

OTHER ITEMS
Bread, whole-wheat, thin sliced (1 loaf)
Chocolate, dark, at least 70 percent cocoa
(1 small bar)

Chocolate chips, dark, at least 70 percent
cocoa (40 g)
Corn tortillas, 15-cm (4)
Hummus (230 g)
Pistachios, unsalted, in-shell (450-g bag)
Pita bread, whole grain (2)
Wine, red, dry

PREP FOR DAYS 1 - 7
You can use these time-saving strategies to set yourself up for success for the week ahead.
Having grab-and-go options throughout the week can be made easier if you prepare these
foods over the weekend.
  • Make Breakfast Egg Bites
  • Make Chocolate-Zucchini Muffins
  • Make Chicken Tortilla Soup
  • Make Oat and Walnut Granola

CALORIES AND CARB ADD-INS
Your meal plan can be customized to meet your specific nutritional requirements and
preferences using these calorie and carb additions. Add-ins with fewer than 5 grams of
carbs are ideal if you feel you need more food without the carbs. Feel free to choose the
add-ins with 10 to 20 grams of carbs if you are okay with more carbs in your daily meals.
This list can be used for all 21 days of your meal plan.

IF EATING UP TO 100 CALORIES WITH 10 TO 20 GRAMS OF CARBS
  • 160 g cooked green peas
  • 350 g raspberries
  • 170 g cooked oatmeal
  • 120 g cooked quinoa
  • 30 g dark chocolate (14 g equals 1
    to 2 squares)

  • 70 g hummus
  • 120 g black beans
  • 250 g cooked winter squash
  • 110 g shelled edamame
  • 170 g plain non-fat Greek yogurt

IF EATING UP TO 100 CALORIES WITH FEWER THAN 5 GRAMS OF CARBS
  • ½ avocado
  • 120 g tofu
  • 460 g non starchy vegetables
  • 30 g to 60 g natural cheese
  • 2 hard-boiled eggs

  • 85 g grilled chicken
  • 2 tablespoons unsalted nuts
  • 110 g cottage cheese
  • 1 tablespoon natural nut butter
  • 1 tablespoon olive or coconut oil

DAY 1

Breakfast	Chocolate-Zucchini Muffin Greek Yogurt Sundae
Snack	70 g walnuts, 1 piece string cheese, and 1/2 apple
Lunch	Chicken Tortilla Soup Cucumber, Tomato, and Avocado Salad
Snack	½ apple with 1 tablespoon almond butter
Dinner	Black Bean Enchilada Skillet Casserole topped with ¼ sliced avocado Spicy Roasted Cauliflower with Lime
Snack	Leftover Chocolate-Zucchini Muffins and 2 tablespoons walnuts

DAY 2

Breakfast	2 Leftover Breakfast Egg Bites Leftover Chocolate-Zucchini Muffins, 120 g plain non-fat Greek yogurt
Snack	110 g blueberries and 1 piece string cheese

Lunch	Leftover Cucumber, Tomato, and Avocado Salad Leftover Black Bean Enchilada Skillet Casserole
Snack	70 g walnuts and 240 g favourite non starchy veggies with 2 tablespoons hummus
Dinner	Easy Chicken Cacciatore Mozzarella and Artichoke Stuffed Spaghetti Squash
Snack	30g pistachios (49 nuts)

DAY 3

Breakfast	1 serving Oat and Walnut Granola 230 g plain non-fat Greek yogurt
Snack	Leftover Chocolate-Zucchini Muffins and 1 piece string cheese
Lunch	Leftover Chicken Tortilla Soup topped with ¼ sliced avocado, 80 g black beans, Leftover Spicy Roasted Cauliflower with Lime
Snack	480 g favourite non starchy vegetables with 70 g hummus
Dinner	Roasted Salmon with Honey-Mustard Sauce 450 g favourite roasted vegetables (cook alongside the salmon) 100 g cooked quinoa
Snack	15 g dark chocolate and 2 tablespoons favourite nuts

Breakfast	2 leftover Breakfast Egg Bites Leftover Chocolate-Zucchini Muffins 140 g plain non-fat Greek yogurt
Snack	70 g walnuts and 120 g favourite berries
Lunch	Leftover Black Bean Enchilada Skillet Casserole topped with ¼ sliced avocado Leftover Spicy Roasted Cauliflower with Lime
Snack	1 small apple with 1 tablespoon almond butter
Dinner	Leftover Easy Chicken Cacciatore Leftover Mozzarella and Artichoke Stuffed Spaghetti Squash
Snack	30g pistachios (49 nuts)

Breakfast
½ Coconut-Berry Sunrise Smoothie
2 leftover Breakfast Egg Bites

Snack
110 g blueberries and 1 piece string cheese

Lunch
Leftover Chicken Tortilla Soup topped with ¼ sliced avocado
80 g black beans
Simple green salad with Ranch Vegetable Dip and Dressing or other healthy dressing

Snack
Leftover Chocolate-Zucchini Muffins and ¼ cup walnuts

Dinner
Leftover Roasted Salmon with Honey-Mustard Sauce
430 g favourite roasted vegetables, 110 g cooked quinoa

Dessert (optional)
Grilled Peach and Coconut Yogurt Bowls

DAY 6

Breakfast
Brussels Sprout Hash and Eggs
220 g favourite berries

Snack
Leftover Chocolate-Zucchini Muffins and 1 piece string cheese

Lunch	Thai Peanut, Carrot, and Shrimp Soup Red Pepper, Goat Cheese, and Arugula Open-Faced Grilled Sandwich
Snack	Leftover Coconut-Berry Sunrise Smoothie
Dinner	Beet, Goat Cheese, and Walnut Pesto with Zoodles
Dessert (optional):	Leftover Grilled Peach and Coconut Yogurt Bowl

DAY 7

Breakfast	Crispy Breakfast Pita with Egg and Canadian Bacon topped with ¼ sliced avocado 120 g favourite berries
Snack	Leftover Brussels Sprout Hash and Eggs
Lunch	Leftover Thai Peanut, Carrot, and Shrimp Soup Red Pepper, Goat Cheese, and Arugula Open-Faced Grilled Sandwich
Snack	1/2 pita bread and 430 g favourite non starchy vegetables with 2 tablespoons Ranch Vegetable Dip and Dressing
Dinner	Whole Veggie-Stuffed Trout
Snack	110 g plain non-fat Greek yogurt with 2 tablespoons crushed walnuts, 1 teaspoon ground cinnamon, and 2 tablespoons favourite berries

Days 8 - 14

Your second week has come! Congratulations! If you are monitoring your blood sugar levels at home, you should notice an improvement as you start the second week. When meals are paired properly, many of my clients are amazed at how satisfying they are, and I hope you are too. The right combination of real foods will lead to success time and time again.

Please remember that this is not a diet. You are simply making sure your body gets the right balance of macronutrients to function optimally, while being cognizant of the type and amount of carbohydrates you consume to help lower your blood sugar levels.

Check in with yourself this week to make sure you're drinking enough water during the day. While the daily meal plans provided include the recommended amount of fibre, many people eat far less fibre before they begin to improve their diet. In addition to allowing your body to digest your food fully, maintaining adequate hydration will increase your mental clarity and energy levels as you proceed.

DAY 8 - 14 SHOPPING LIST

FRESH PRODUCE

Apples (2)
Asparagus (450 g)
Arugula (25 g)
Avocados (3)
Bean sprouts (110 g)
Bell peppers, red (4)
Berries, mixed (950 g)
Blueberries (440 g)
Broccoli (4 heads)
Cabbage, green (1 small head)
Carrots (1 bunch)
Celery (1 bunch)
Coriander, fresh (1 bunch)
Dill, fresh (1 bunch)
Fruit of choice (2)
Garlic (3 heads)
Ginger (1 small knob)
Kale, baby (280 g)
Leafy greens such as kale and/or spinach (55 g)
Lemons (2)
Lettuce, leaf (2 heads)
Limes (2)
Mango (1)
Mushrooms, brown (570 g)
Onion, red (1)
Onion, white (1)
Onions, yellow (6)
Parsley, fresh (1 bunch)

Pepper, jalapeño (1)
Scallions (1 bunch)
Spinach (3 bunches)
Squash, delicata (1)
Sweet potatoes (4)
Tomatoes (1 small, 1 large)
Tomatoes, cherry (440 g)
Vegetables for snacking such as cauliflower, radishes, cucumbers, bell peppers (2,4 kg)

CANNED AND BOTTLED ITEMS

Almond milk, unsweetened, plain (4 ¾ dl)
Artichoke hearts (1 [400-g] can)
Beef broth, low sodium (9 ½ dl)
Coconut milk, unsweetened, plain (4 ¾ dl)
Pesto (56 g)
Tomatoes, crushed (1 [790-g] can)
Tomatoes, whole (1 [790-g] can)
Tomato paste (3 [170-g] cans)
Tuna, chunk light, packed in water (1 [140-g] can)
Vegetable broth, low sodium (9 ½ dl)

FROZEN FOODS

Berries, mixed (450 g)
Cauliflower (450 g)
Spinach (1 [280-g] package)

DAIRY AND EGGS
Cheese, cheddar, shredded (55 g)
Cheese, mozzarella, shredded (25 g)
Cheese, natural, any type (85 g)
Cheese, string (3 pieces)
Eggs (12)
Goat cheese, crumbled (85 g)
Greek yogurt, plain, non-fat (460 g)
Yogurt, unsweetened, vanilla, non-fat
(170 g)

MEAT AND FISH
Beef stew meat (450 g)

Chicken breast, cooked (340 g)
Salmon fillet (450 g)
Tilapia (230 g)
Turkey, lean, ground (450 g)

OTHER ITEMS
Bread, whole-wheat, thin sliced (1 loaf)
Chocolate, dark, at least 70 percent cocoa
(1 small bar)
Flatbread, whole-wheat (2)
Hummus (230 g)
Tortilla, 20-cm, whole-wheat, low carb
(4)

PREP FOR DAYS 8 - 14
- Make Leftover Spinach, Artichoke, and Goat Cheese Breakfast Bake
- Make tuna salad for Tomato Tuna Melts
- Bake sweet potatoes
- Make Tomato and Kale Soup
- Make Ranch Vegetable Dip and Dressing
- Make Easy Italian Dressing

THE MEAL PLAN

DAY 8

Breakfast	2 servings Spinach, Artichoke, and Goat Cheese Breakfast Bake
Snack	1 small baked sweet potato topped with 2 tablespoons crushed nuts (almonds, pecans, walnuts)
Lunch	430 g favourite non starchy vegetables with ⅔ dl Quick Guacamole
Snack	Tomato Tuna Melts

Dinner	Tomato and Kale Soup

Snack	110 g berries and 70 g walnuts

DAY 9

Breakfast	1 serving Oat and Walnut Granola

Snack	230 g plain non-fat Greek yogurt

Lunch	220 g berries and 1 piece string cheese

Snack	Leftover Lentil Loaf

Dinner	Simple green salad with Ranch Vegetable Dip and Dressing

Snack	½ apple with 2 tablespoons almond butter

DAY 10

Breakfast	2 servings Spinach, Artichoke, and Goat Cheese Breakfast Bake
Snack	½ Coconut-Berry Sunrise Smoothie
Lunch	430 g favourite non starchy vegetables with ⅔ dl Quick Guacamole
Snack	Leftover Tomato Tuna Melt
Dinner	Leftover Tomato and Kale Soup
Snack	1 apple with 2 tablespoons almond butter

DAY 11

Breakfast	2 servings leftover Spinach, Artichoke, and Goat Cheese Breakfast Bake
Snack	1 small baked sweet potato topped with cinnamon and 2 tablespoons crushed nuts (pecans, walnuts, almonds)
Lunch	Leftover Coconut-Berry Sunrise Smoothie

Snack	Leftover Beef and Mushroom Barley Soup
Dinner	Simple green salad with Easy Italian Dressing
Snack	70 g walnuts and 1 piece string cheese

DAY 12

Breakfast	Avocado and Goat Cheese Toast topped with 1 poached egg
Snack	110 g berries
Lunch	Leftover Tomato and Kale Soup
Snack	Leftover Lentil Loaf
Dinner	Simple green salad with Easy Italian Dressing
Snack	1 piece string cheese and 1 small fruit of choice

DAY 13

Breakfast	2 servings Sweet Potato, Onion, and Turkey Sausage Hash
Snack	Hard-boiled or poached egg
Lunch	Leftover Tomato and Kale Soup
Snack	Thai-Style Chicken Roll-Ups
Dinner	Simple green salad with Easy Italian Dressing
Dessert (optional)	30 g natural cheese and 230 g sliced vegetables with 2 tablespoons hummus

DAY 14

Breakfast	Leftover Sweet Potato, Onion, and Turkey Sausage Hash
Snack	430 g vegetables with 80 g Quick Guacamole
Lunch	Leftover Thai-Style Chicken Roll-Up
Snack	1 small fruit of choice
Dinner	Simple green salad with Easy Italian Dressing
Snack	110 g plain non-fat Greek yogurt with 2 tablespoons crushed walnuts, 1 teaspoon cinnamon, and 2 tablespoons berries

Days 15 - 21

It's the final stretch now, and I hope your self-esteem is starting to grow! Take pride in how you have implemented a new way of eating to better your long-term health through your success thus far. It's okay if you haven't followed the meal plans exactly. In order to achieve results, you do not need to eat perfectly; you just need to improve on your starting point and keep going. Success depends on consistency and balance.

You should be able to identify by now your new favourite meals, snacks, and foods that you enjoy and that you know won't raise your blood sugar levels. If you know these are your go-to choices throughout your diabetes journey, you'll use them again and again with confidence.

Make sure you acknowledge the physical and emotional changes you are experiencing. Notes and observations can be made in the meal plan if you find it helpful, since it is yours to customize.

DAY 15 - 21 SHOPPING LIST

FRESH PRODUCE

Apples (2)
Asparagus (450 g)
Avocados (3)
Basil, fresh (1 bunch)
Bell peppers, red (4)
Berries, mixed (950 g)
Blueberries (460 g)
Brussels sprouts (450 g)
Cabbage, green (1 small head)
Cabbage, red (1 small head)
Carrots (2 bunches)
Celery (1 bunch)
Coriander, fresh (1 bunch)
Cucumbers (2)
Garlic (2 heads)
Ginger (1 small knob)
Jicama (1 small)
Leafy greens such as kale and/or spinach (55 g)
Lemons (4)
Lettuce, leaf (2 heads)
Lettuce, romaine hearts (2 heads)
Limes (3)
Mango (1)
Mint, fresh (1 bunch)
Mushrooms, brown (55 g)
Onion, red (1)
Onions, yellow (2)
Pear (1)
Peppers, jalapeño (2)

Salad greens, mixed (280 g)
Scallions (2 bunches)
Spinach (1 bunch)
Spinach, baby (28 g)
Sweet potato (1)
Tomatillos (230 g)
Tomato (1)
Tomatoes, cherry (460 g)
Vegetables for snacking such as cauliflower, radishes, cucumbers, bell peppers (1.7 L)

DAIRY AND EGGS

Butter (110 g)
Cheese, natural, any variety (25 g)
Cheese, Parmesan, grated (140 g)
Cheese, string (3 pieces)
Cottage cheese, low-fat (230 g)
Eggs (18)
Goat cheese, crumbled (55 g)
Greek yogurt, plain, non-fat (950 g)
Yogurt, unsweetened, vanilla, non-fat (170 g)

CANNED AND BOTTLED ITEMS

Almond milk, unsweetened, plain (4 ¾ dl)
Black beans, low-sodium (1 [430-g] can)
Coconut milk, canned (1 [430-g] can)
Chickpeas, low-sodium (1 [430-g] can)

Coconut milk, unsweetened, plain (4 ¾ dl)
Sun-dried tomatoes (15 g)
Tomato paste (2 [170-g] cans)
Tomatoes, whole (1 [790-g] can)
Tuna, chunk light, packed in water (1 [140-g] can)
Vegetable broth, low sodium (9 ½ dl)
White beans, low-sodium (1 [430-g] can)

MEAT AND FISH
Canadian bacon (25 g)
Chicken breast, boneless, skinless (1 [230-g] breast)

Protein, lean, any type (230 g)
Salmon (4 [110-g] fillets)
Sea scallops (450 g)
Shrimp, peeled, deveined (450 g)
Turkey, lean, ground (230 g)
Turkey, sliced (25 g) (optional)

OTHER ITEMS
Bread, whole-wheat, thin sliced (1 loaf)
Chocolate, dark, at least 70 percent cocoa (1 small bar)
Dinner rolls, whole-wheat (4)
Pita bread, whole-wheat (4)
Wine, white, dry

PREP FOR DAYS 15 - 21
- Make Breakfast Egg Bites
- Make hummus for Tuna, Hummus, and Veggie Wraps
- Make Curried Carrot Soup
- Make Easy Italian Dressing

THE MEAL PLAN

DAY 15	
Breakfast	2 Breakfast Egg Bites in whole-wheat pita with a handful of favourite greens
Snack	½ Coconut-Berry Sunrise Smoothie
Lunch	½ apple with 1 tablespoon almond butter
Snack	Tuna, Hummus, and Veggie Wraps with 2 slices avocado

Dinner	Curried Carrot Soup
Snack	½ apple and 1 piece string cheese

DAY 16

Breakfast	Greek Yogurt Sundae
Snack	1 serving Oat and Walnut Granola
Lunch	70 g walnuts
Snack	Leftover Tuna, Hummus, and Veggie Wraps with 2 slices avocado
Dinner	Leftover Curried Carrot Soup
Snack	Leftover Coconut-Berry Sunrise Smoothie

DAY 17

Breakfast	2 leftover Breakfast Egg Bites
Snack	110 g blueberries and 110g plain non-fat Greek yogurt
Lunch	1 serving Oat and Walnut Granola
Snack	2 tablespoons leftover hummus with 220 g cut vegetables
Dinner	Leftover Barbecue Turkey Burger Sliders, 1 baked sweet potato with 1 teaspoon olive oil, Simple green salad with Easy Italian Dressing
Snack	1 piece string cheese and 1 small pear

DAY 18

Breakfast	Avocado and Goat Cheese Toast
Snack	2 leftover Breakfast Egg Bites

Lunch	2 tablespoons leftover hummus with 210 g cut vegetables
Snack	Leftover Roasted Salmon with Salsa Verde
Dinner	Leftover Rainbow Black Bean Salad
Snack	Simple green salad with Easy Italian Dressing

DAY 19

Breakfast	1 serving Oat and Walnut Granola with 230 g plain non-fat Greek yogurt
Snack	½ apple with 1 tablespoon almond butter
Lunch	Leftover Chicken Caesar Salad
Snack	2 tablespoons hummus with 1 whole-wheat pita
Dinner	60 g nuts of choice

Snack	Leftover Shrimp Burgers with Fruity Salsa and Salad

DAY 20

Breakfast	Gluten-Free Carrot and Oat Pancakes
Snack	1 scrambled egg
Lunch	110 g berries and 80 g favourite nuts
Snack	Leftover Chicken Caesar Salad
Dinner	110 g favourite grilled protein, 110 g starch (quinoa, beans), and 450 g vegetables with 2 tablespoons Easy Italian Dressing
Dessert (optional)	1 or 2 leftover Chocolate Peanut Butter Freezer Bites

DAY 21

Breakfast	Brussels Sprout Hash and Eggs
Snack	230 g berries
Lunch:	1 slice Canadian bacon
Snack	½ recipe Coconut-Berry Sunrise Smoothie
Dinner	Leftover Crispy Parmesan Cups with White Beans and Veggies
Snack	110 g favourite lean protein

Measurement Conversions

It is important to note that it is virtually impossible to include an all-inclusive conversion table as all foods have slightly different measurements when converted.

KITCHEN CONVERSIONS

LIQUID CONVERSIONS

1/4 TSP	=	1 ML		
1/2 TSP	=	2 ML		
1 TSP	=	5 ML		
3 TSP	=	1 TBL	= 1/2 FL OZ	= 15 ML
2 TBLS	=	1/8 CUP	= 1 FL OZ	= 30 ML
4 TBLS	=	1/4 CUP	= 2 FL OZ	= 60 ML
5 1/3 TBLS	=	1/3 CUP	= 3 FL OZ	= 80 ML
8 TBLS	=	1/2 CUP	= 4 FL OZ	= 120 ML
10 2/3	=	2/3 CUP	= 5 FL OZ	= 160 ML
12 TBLS	=	3/4 CUP	= 6 FL OZ	= 180 ML
16 TBLS	=	1 CUP	= 8 FL OZ	= 240 ML
1 PT	=	2 CUPS	= 16 FL OZ	= 480 ML
1 QT	=	4 CUPS	= 32 FL OZ	= 960 ML
33 FL OZ	=	1000 ML	= 1 L	

Length

METRIC	IMPERIAL
3mm	1/8 inch
6mm	1/4 inch
2.5cm	1 inch
3cm	1 1/4 inch
5cm	2 inches
10cm	4 inches
15cm	6 inches
20cm	8 inches
22.5cm	9 inches
25cm	10 inches
28cm	11 inches

Oven Temperatures

	Fahrenheit	Celsius	Gas Mark
Freezing Water	32°F	0°C	
Room Temp.	68°F	20°C	
Boiling Water	212° F	100°C	
Baking	325° F	160°C	3
	350° F	180°C	4
	375° F	190°C	5
	400° F	200°C	6
	425° F	220°C	7
	450° F	230°C	8
Broiling			Grill

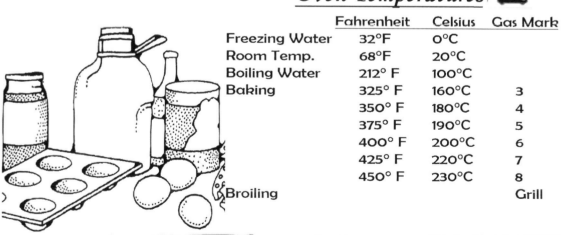

Weight Conversions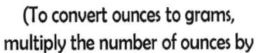

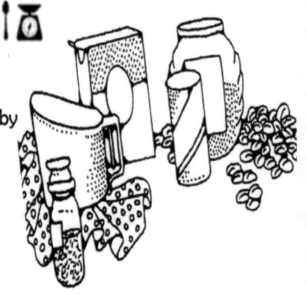

(To convert ounces to grams,
multiply the number of ounces by
30.)

1 oz	=	1/16 lb	=	30 g
4 oz	=	1/4 lb	=	120 g
8 oz	=	1/2 lb	=	240 g
12 oz	=	3/4 lb	=	360 g
16 oz	=	1 lb	=	480 g

Conversions for Different Types of Food

Standard Cup	Fine Powder (like flour)	Grains (like rice)	Granular (like sugar)	Liquid Solids (like butter)	Liquid (eg. milk)
1	140 g	150 g	190 g	200 g	240 ml
3/4	105 g	113 g	143 g	150 g	180 ml
2/3	93 g	100 g	125 g	133 g	160 ml
1/2	70 g	75 g	95 g	100 g	120 ml
1/3	47 g	50 g	63 g	67 g	80 ml
1/4	35 g	38 g	48 g	50 g	60 ml
1/8	18 g	19 g	24 g	25 g	30 ml

Breakfast Recipes

Kickstart Your Day Berry Smoothie

Serves:2	Type 1	Prep:20 mins.	Cook: 0 mins.

Nutrition per Serving:

263 calories	3 g fat	50 g carbs	15g protein

Ingredients:
- ❖ Orange (2)
- ❖ Greek yogurt (285g)
- ❖ Banana (2 small, peeled)
- ❖ Strawberries (650g)
- ❖ Flaxseeds (1.5 tsp)

Directions:
1. Cut the orange in half and remove the pit. Cube the pulp.
2. Place the ingredients in a food processor. Process until the ingredients are combined.
3. Serve immediately, or chill for an hour before serving.

Avocado and Goat Cheese Toast

Serves:2	Type 2	Prep:5 mins.	Cook: 0 mins.

Nutrition per Serving:

137 calories	6 g fat	18 g carbs	5g protein

Ingredients:

- ❖ Whole-wheat thin-sliced bread (2 slices)
- ❖ Avocado (½)
- ❖ Goat cheese (2 tbsp., crumbled)
- ❖ Salt (to taste)

Directions:

1. In a toaster or broiler, toast the bread until browned.
2. Remove the flesh from the avocado. In a medium bowl, use a fork to mash the avocado flesh. Use it to spread onto your toast.
3. To with a sprinkle of goat cheese and season to taste.
4. Add any toppings and serve.

Buckwheat Pancakes

Serves: 2	Type 1	Prep: 20 mins.	Cook: 10 mins.

Nutrition per Serving:

626 calories	11 g fat	110 g carbs	31g protein

Ingredients:
- Egg (2)
- Baking soda (1/2 tsp)
- Baking powder (2 tsp)
- Buttermilk (625ml)
- Buckwheat flour (280g)
- Honey (30ml)
- Vanilla extract (7.5ml)
- Salt (pinch)
- Clarified ghee (30g)

Directions:
1. Mix in a bowl, buckwheat flour, baking powder, soda, salt, and honey.
2. In a separate bowl, add all wet ingredients and whisk together.
3. Combine dry and wet ingredients to form a thick, smooth batter. Let it rest for 15 minutes.
4. Heat a skillet and add some olive oil.
5. In the centre of the skillet, pour a large spoonful of batter a few inches in diameter and less than an inch in thickness.
6. When the batter starts bubbling over. This indicates it is time to flip it.
7. Flip the pancake and cook on both sides, pouring some more olive oil if needed to prevent sticking.
8. Pancake is done once it is brown, in about 2-3 minutes. Repeat these steps for the remaining batter.
9. Serve the pancakes warm with honey, fruit, or honey.

Couscous

Serves:5   Type 1   Prep:20 mins.   Cook: 15 mins.

Nutrition per Serving:

426 calories   11g fat   62g carbs   21g protein

Ingredients:

- ❖ Whole-Wheat Couscous (450g, Uncooked)
- ❖ Skim Milk (2.1 L)
- ❖ 5 cm Cinnamon Stick (3)
- ❖ Honey (90 ml)
- ❖ Pinch Of Salt
- ❖ Olive Oil (60 ml, Divided)
- ❖ Raisins And Currants (120g)
- ❖ Dried Apricots (350g)

Directions:

1. In a medium pan, combine cinnamon and milk and let boil for 3 minutes, stirring constantly.
2. Remove from heat; add the couscous, dried fruits, currants and salt, and 4 tsp of honey to the pan. Mix well.
3. Cover and set aside for 15 minutes.
4. Pour into 4 serving bowls and add 1 tsp olive oil and ½ tsp honey on top of each bowl. Stir and serve immediately.

Gluten-Free Carrot and Oat Pancakes

Serves:4	Type 2	Prep:10 mins.	Cook: 20 mins.

Nutrition per Serving:

226 calories	8 g fat	24 g carbs	15g protein

Ingredients:

- Rolled oats (90 g)
- Carrots (230g shredded)
- Cottage cheese (200g low-fat)
- Eggs (2)
- Almond milk (1 ⅛ dl, unsweetened plain)
- Baking powder (1 tsp.)

- Ground cinnamon (½ tsp.)
- Ground flaxseed (2 tbsp.)
- Greek yogurt (⅔ dl plain non-fat)
- Pure honey (1 tbsp.)
- Canola oil (2 tsp., divided)

Directions:

1. In a blender jar, process the oats until they resemble flour. Add the carrots, cottage cheese, eggs, almond milk, baking powder, cinnamon, and flaxseed to the jar. Process until smooth.
2. In a small bowl, combine the yogurt and honey and stir well. Set aside.
3. In a large skillet, heat 1 teaspoon of oil over medium heat. Using a measuring cup, add ⅔ dl of batter per pancake to the skillet.
4. Cook for 1 to 2 minutes until bubbles form on the surface and flip the pancakes.
5. Cook for another minute until the pancakes are browned and cooked through.
6. Repeat with the remaining 1 teaspoon of oil and remaining batter. Serve warm topped with the honey yogurt.

Oatmeal with Fruits & Nuts

Serves:5	Type 1	Prep:15 mins.	Cook: 15 mins.

Nutrition per Serving:

211 calories	1 g fat	40 g carbs	10g protein

Ingredients:
- Oats (600g, raw)
- Skim milk or water (1.2 L)
- Cinnamon (1 ¼ tsp)
- Peach (1, chopped)
- Handful of raisins
- Dried cranberries (300g)
- Assorted nuts, blanched and slivered to sprinkle on top
- Honey (2 ½ tsp., optional)

Directions:
1. Cook the oats as per instructions then add the remaining ingredients.
2. Add seasonal fruits and nuts to enhance the flavour of the oatmeal.
3. Add blueberries, strawberries, and honey for a more classic combination. Enjoy!

Greek Yogurt Bowl

Serves:2	Type 1	Prep:15 mins.	Cook: 0 mins.

Nutrition per Serving:

387 calories	9 g fat	76 g carbs	10g protein

Ingredients:
- Greek yogurt (400g, plain)
- Raspberries (230g)
- Strawberries (6, hulled and sliced)
- Blueberries (200g, fresh)
- Organic honey (4 tbsp, raw)

Directions:
1. Place Greek yogurt in a bowl. Add the sliced banana and berries.
2. Drizzle honey on top. Top with seeds and nuts of your choice (if desired).
3. Serve chilled.

Mediterranean Omelette with Wheat Bread & Blueberries

Serves:2	Type 1	Prep:20 mins.	Cook: 7 mins.

Nutrition per Serving:

428 calories	35 g fat	24 g carbs	9g protein

Ingredients:

- ❖ Eggs (4, large)
- ❖ Olive oil (4 tbsp, extra virgin)
- ❖ Yellow onion (2 medium, chopped)
- ❖ Garlic (2 cloves, minced)
- ❖ Spinach (460g, chopped)
- ❖ Tomato (1 medium, diced)
- ❖ Skim milk (4 tbsp)

- ❖ Kalamata olives (8, pitted and diced)
- ❖ Salt and pepper (to taste)
- ❖ Feta cheese (6 tbsp, crumbled)
- ❖ Fresh parsley (2 tbsp, chopped)

For Serving:
- ❖ Whole Wheat Bread (4 slices)
- ❖ Blueberries (220g)
- ❖ Skim Milk/Coffee (4 ¾ dl)

Directions:

1. Heat the oil in a pan. Add onions to the pan and fry until brown. Then, add garlic and fry for 2 minutes.
2. Add the salt, spinach, tomatoes, and cook for a few minutes. In a bowl, add egg and milk and whisk together.
3. Add the pepper and olives to the frying pan and pour the egg mixture over the sautéed vegetables.
4. Spread it around and turn up the heat so the egg cooks quickly.
5. You can lift the omelette a bit to allow the upper liquid layer to go underneath the cooked egg.
6. Continue cooking until the egg is cooked. Fold the omelette in half. Transfer to a plate, add freshly chopped parsley and cheese.
7. Serve warm with 2 slices of Whole Wheat Bread, 1 ⅛ dl Blueberries, and 1 Glass of Milk/Coffee.

Simple Mediterranean Breakfast With Sashimi & Pickles

Serves:5	Type 1	Prep:15 mins.	Cook: 0 mins.

Nutrition per Serving:

215 calories	11 g fat	18 g carbs	12g protein

Ingredients:

- Ricotta Cheese (200g, Fresh)
- Salmon (430g, sashimi grade, thinly sliced)
- Eggs (5)
- Green Olives (5)
- Sourdough Rye Bread (5 Slice)
- Fresh Pickles (15 Slices)
- Olive Oil (3 1/3 Tsp)
- Sea Salt And Fresh Black Pepper (To Taste)

Directions:

1. Boil your eggs and slice your salmon.
2. Spread the ricotta on the bread, each slice top with a sliced egg, salmon, pickle slices, and an olive.
3. Drizzle with olive oil then seasons with salt and pepper. Enjoy!

Breakfast Egg Bites

| Serves:8 | Type 2 | Prep:10 mins. | Cook: 25 mins. |

Nutrition per Serving:

| 67 calories | 4 g fat | 3 g carbs | 6g protein |

Ingredients:

- ❖ Non-stick cooking spray
- ❖ Eggs (6, beaten)
- ❖ Milk (⅔ dl unsweetened plain almond)
- ❖ Red bell pepper (1, diced)
- ❖ Spinach (200g, chopped)
- ❖ Goat cheese (80g, crumbled)

- ❖ Brown mushrooms (150g, sliced)
- ❖ Sun-dried tomatoes (70g, sliced)
- ❖ Salt (to taste)
- ❖ Freshly ground black pepper (to taste)

Directions:

1. Preheat the oven to 180 °C. Spray 8 muffin cups of a 2.8-L muffin tin with non-stick cooking spray. Set aside.
2. In a large mixing bowl, combine the eggs, almond milk, bell pepper, spinach, goat cheese, mushrooms, and tomatoes. Season with salt and pepper.
3. Fill the prepared muffin cups three-fourths full with the egg mixture.
4. Bake for 20 to 25 minutes until the eggs are set. Let cool slightly and remove the egg bites from the muffin tin.
5. Serve warm, or store in an airtight container in the refrigerator for up to 5 days or in the freezer for up to 1 month.

Italian Omelette

| Serves:5 | Type 1 | Prep:15 mins. | Cook: 10 mins. |

Nutrition per Serving:

| 773 calories | 75 g fat | 7 g carbs | 25g protein |

Ingredients:

- Mushrooms (640g, Sliced)
- Zucchini (1kg, Sliced)
- Olive Oil (15 Tbsp, Divided)
- Eggs (20)
- Water (15 Tbsp)
- Salt and Pepper
- Mozzarella (120g)

- **For the Sauce:**
- Olive Oil (5 Tbsp)
- Parsley (10 Tbsp, Chopped)
- Tomato (5 Medium)
- Garlic (5 cloves)
- Salt (A Pinch)
- Basil (2 ½ Tsp)

Directions:

1. Heat 1 tbsp of olive oil in a skillet, then add the mushroom and zucchini. Sauté until brown. Set aside but keep warm.
2. In a bowl, whisk together eggs, water, salt, and pepper. Heat the skillet and add the remaining 2 tbsp oil.
3. Add the beaten eggs. Cook for a few minutes. As the eggs cook, push the uncooked portion beneath and let the top part set.
4. Once the eggs are cooked, add the vegetables over to one side and sprinkle the mozzarella cheese.
5. Fold the other half of the egg over the filling. Remove the eggs on a plate.
6. When making the sauce, heat oil. Add basil, tomatoes, parsley, and garlic. Cook thoroughly until done.
7. Serve the sauce with the omelette. Enjoy!

Coconut-Berry Sunrise Smoothie

Serves: 2	Type 2	Prep: 5 mins.	Cook: 0 mins.

Nutrition per Serving:

181 calories	15 g fat	8 g carbs	6g protein

Ingredients:
- ❖ Mixed berries (80g)
- ❖ Ground flaxseed (1 tbsp.)
- ❖ Unsweetened coconut flakes (2 tbsp.)
- ❖ Unsweetened plain coconut milk (1 ⅛ dl)
- ❖ Leafy greens (50g, kale and spinach)
- ❖ Vanilla non-fat yogurt (80g unsweetened)
- ❖ Ice (1 dl)

Directions:
1. In a blender jar, combine the berries, flaxseed, coconut flakes, coconut milk, greens, yogurt, and ice.
2. Process until smooth. Serve.

Greek Yogurt Sundae

Serves: 1   Type 2   Prep: 5 mins.   Cook: 0 mins.

Nutrition per Serving:

237 calories   11 g fat   16 g carbs   21g protein

Ingredients:

- Greek yogurt (70g, plain non-fat)
- Mixed berries (30g)
- Cashew (2 tbsp.)
- Ground flaxseed (1 tbsp.)
- Mint leaves (2 fresh, shredded)

Directions:
1. Spoon the yogurt into a small bowl. Top with the berries, nuts, and flaxseed. Garnish with the mint and serve.

Crispy Breakfast Pita with Egg and Bacon

Serves: 2   Type 2   Prep: 5 mins.   Cook: 15 mins.

Nutrition per Serving:

250 calories   14 g fat   10 g carbs   13g protein

Ingredients:

- Pita bread (1, whole grain)
- Extra-virgin olive oil (3 tsp., divided)
- Eggs (2)
- Bacon slices (2)
- Juice of ½ lemon
- Microgreens (50g)
- Goat cheese (2 tbsp. Crumbled)
- Ground black pepper (2 tbsp., crumbled)

Directions:
1. Heat a large skillet over medium heat. Cut the pita bread in half and brush each side of both halves with ¼ teaspoon of olive oil (using a total of 1 teaspoon oil).
2. Cook for 2 to 3 minutes on each side, then remove from the skillet.
3. In the same skillet, heat 1 teaspoon of oil over medium heat. Crack the eggs into the skillet and cook until the eggs are set, 2 to 3 minutes. Remove from the skillet.
4. In the same skillet, cook the Canadian bacon for 3 to 5 minutes, flipping once.
5. In a large bowl, whisk together the remaining 1 teaspoon of oil and the lemon juice. Add the microgreens and toss to combine.
6. Top each pita half with half of the microgreens, 1 piece of bacon, 1 egg, and 1 tbsp. of goat cheese. Season with pepper and serve.

Oat and Walnut Granola

| Serves:16 | Type 2 | Prep:10 mins. | Cook: 30 mins. |

Nutrition per Serving:

| 224 calories | 15 g fat | 20 g carbs | 5g protein |

Ingredients:

- Rolled oats (340 g)
- Walnut pieces (210g)
- Pepitas (110 g)
- Salt (¼ tsp.)
- Ground cinnamon (1 tsp.)

- Ground ginger (1 tsp.)
- Coconut oil (1 ⅛ dl, melted)
- Unsweetened applesauce (1 ⅛ dl)
- Vanilla extract (1 tsp.)
- Cherries (110g, dried)

Directions:

1. Preheat the oven to 180 ºC. Line a baking sheet with parchment paper.
2. In a large bowl, toss the oats, walnuts, pepitas, salt, cinnamon, and ginger.
3. In a large measuring cup, combine the coconut oil, applesauce, and vanilla. Pour over the dry mixture and mix well.
4. Transfer the mixture to the prepared baking sheet. Cook for 30 minutes, stirring about halfway through.
5. Remove from the oven and let the granola sit undisturbed until completely cool.
6. Break the granola into pieces and stir in the dried cherries.
7. Transfer to an airtight container, and store at room temperature for up to 2 weeks.

Chocolate-Zucchini Muffins

Serves:12   Type 2   Prep:15 mins.   Cook: 20 mins.

Nutrition per Serving:

121 calories   7 g fat   16 g carbs   2g protein

Ingredients:

- ❖ Zucchini (350g, grated)
- ❖ Rolled oats (130g)
- ❖ Ground cinnamon (1 tsp.)
- ❖ Baking powder (2 tsp.)
- ❖ Salt (¼ tsp.)
- ❖ Egg (1 large)

- ❖ Vanilla extract (1 tsp.)
- ❖ Coconut oil (⅔ dl, melted)
- ❖ Unsweetened applesauce (1 ⅛ dl)
- ❖ Honey (70g)
- ❖ Dark chocolate chips (80g)

Directions:

1. Preheat the oven to 180 °C. Grease the cups of a 2.8-L muffin tin or line with paper baking liners. Set aside.
2. Place the zucchini in a colander over the sink to drain.
3. In a blender jar, process the oats until they resemble flour. Transfer to a medium mixing bowl and add the cinnamon, baking powder, and salt. Mix well.
4. In another large mixing bowl, combine the egg, vanilla, coconut oil, applesauce, and honey. Stir to combine.
5. Press the zucchini into the colander, draining any liquids, and add to the wet mixture.
6. Stir the dry mixture into the wet mixture and mix until no dry spots remain. Fold in the chocolate chips.
7. Transfer the batter to the muffin tin, filling each cup a little over halfway.
8. Cook for 16 to 18 minutes until the muffins are lightly browned and a toothpick inserted in the centre comes out clean.
9. Store in an airtight container, refrigerated, for up to 5 days.

Brussels Sprout Hash and Eggs

Serves:4   Type 2   Prep:15 mins.   Cook: 15 mins.
Nutrition per Serving:
158 calories   9 g fat   12 g carbs   10g protein

Ingredients:

- Extra-virgin olive oil (3 tsp., divided)
- Brussels sprouts (450g, sliced)
- Garlic cloves (2, thinly sliced)
- Salt (¼ tsp.)
- Juice of 1 lemon
- Eggs (4)

Directions:

1. In a large skillet, heat 1½ teaspoons of oil over medium heat. Add the Brussels sprouts and toss.
2. Cook, stirring regularly, for 6 to 8 minutes until browned and softened. Add the garlic and continue to cook until fragrant, about 1 minute. Season with the salt and lemon juice. Transfer to a serving dish.
3. 5 cm the same pan, heat the remaining 1.5 teaspoons of oil over medium-high heat.
4. Crack the eggs into the pan. Fry for 2 to 4 minutes, flip, and continue cooking to desired doneness. Serve over the bed of hash.

Spinach, Artichoke, and Goat Cheese Breakfast Bake

Serves:8	Type 2	Prep:10 mins.	Cook: 35 mins.

Nutrition per Serving:

104 calories	5 g fat	6 g carbs	9g protein

Ingredients:

- ❖ Non-stick cooking spray
- ❖ Spinach (1 (280g) package frozen, thawed and drained)
- ❖ Artichoke hearts (1 can, 400g, drained)
- ❖ Red bell pepper (100g, finely, chopped)
- ❖ Garlic cloves (2, minced)
- ❖ Eggs (8, lightly beaten)
- ❖ Almond milk (⅔ dl, unsweetened plain)
- ❖ Salt (½ tsp.)
- ❖ Ground black pepper (½ tsp.)
- ❖ Goat cheese (140g, crumbled)

Directions:

1. Preheat the oven to 190 °C. Spray a 20 cm x 20 cm baking dish with non-stick cooking spray.
2. In a large mixing bowl, combine the spinach, artichoke hearts, bell pepper, garlic, eggs, almond milk, salt, and pepper. Stir well to combine.
3. Transfer the mixture to the baking dish. Sprinkle with the goat cheese.
4. Bake for 35 minutes until the eggs are set. Serve warm.

Roasted Beet Salad with Ricotta Cheese

Serves:4	Type 1	Prep:10 mins.	Cook: 1 hr.

Nutrition per Serving:

290 calories	6 g fat	12 g carbs	6g protein

Ingredients:

- ❖ Red beets (250g, large, wrapped in foil)
- ❖ Yellow beets (250g, small, wrapped in foil)
- ❖ Mesclun (120g)
- ❖ Mustard Vinaigrette (120g)
- ❖ Ricotta cheese (60g)
- ❖ Walnuts (10g, chopped)

Directions:
1. Bake at 200 °C until the beets are tender, about 1 hour.
2. Cool the beets slightly. Trim the root and stem ends and pull off the peels.
3. Cut the red beets crosswise into thin slices.
4. Cut the yellow beets vertically into quarters.
5. Arrange the sliced red beets in circles on cold salad plates. Toss the mesclun with half the vinaigrette.
6. Drizzle the remaining vinaigrette over the sliced beets.
7. Place a small mound of greens in the centre of each plate.
8. Arrange the quartered yellow beets around the greens.
9. Sprinkle the tops of the salads with the crumbled ricotta and walnuts (if using).

Cioppino (Seafood and Tomato Stew)

| Serves:4 | Type 2 | Prep:10 mins. | Cook: 15 mins. |

Nutrition per Serving:

| 242 calories | 8 g fat | 11 g carbs | 23g protein |

Ingredients:

- ❖ Extra-virgin olive oil (2 tbsp.)
- ❖ Onion (1, chopped finely)
- ❖ Garlic clove (1, minced)
- ❖ Dry white wine (1 ⅛ dl)
- ❖ Tomato sauce (1 can, 400g)
- ❖ Shrimp (230g, peeled and deveined)
- ❖ Cod (230g, pin bones removed and cut into 3-cm pieces)
- ❖ Italian seasoning (1 tbsp.)
- ❖ Sea salt (½ tsp.)
- ❖ Pinch red pepper flakes

Directions:

1. Heat the olive oil in a large skillet over medium-high heat until it shimmers.
2. Toss in the onion and cook for 3 minutes, stirring occasionally, or until the onion is translucent.
3. Stir in the garlic and cook for 30 seconds until fragrant.
4. Add the wine and cook for 1 minute, stirring continuously. Stir in the tomato sauce and bring the mixture to a simmer.
5. Add the shrimp and cod, Italian seasoning, salt, and red pepper flakes, and whisk to combine.
6. Continue simmering for about 5 minutes, or until the fish is cooked through.
7. Remove from the heat and serve on plates.

Baked Fish with Tomatoes and Mushrooms

Serves:4   Type 1   Prep:12 mins.   Cook: 25 mins.

Nutrition per Serving:

350 calories   9 g fat   6 g carbs   55g protein

Ingredients:

- Fish (4, whole and small, 340g each)
- Salt (to taste)
- Pepper (to taste)
- Dried thyme (pinch)
- Parsley (4 sprigs)
- Olive oil (as needed)
- Onion (110g, small dice)
- Shallots (30g, minced)
- Mushrooms (230g, chopped)
- Tomato concasse (180g)
- Dry white wine (95 ml)

Directions:

1. Scale and clean the fish but leaves the heads on. Season the fish inside and out with salt and pepper and put a small pinch of thyme and a sprig of parsley in the cavity of each.
2. Use as many baking pans as possible to hold the fish in a single layer. Oil the pans with a little olive oil.
3. Sauté the onions and shallots in a little olive oil about 1 minute. Add the mushrooms and sauté lightly.
4. Put the sautéed vegetables and the tomatoes in the bottoms of the baking pans. Put the fish in the pans. Oil the tops lightly. Pour in the wine.
5. Bake at 200 ºC until the fish is done. The time will vary but will average 15-20 minutes. Base often with the liquid in the pan.
6. Remove the fish and keep them warm until they are plated.
7. Remove the vegetables from the pans with a slotted spoon and check for seasonings. Serve a spoonful of the vegetables with the fish, placing it under or alongside each fish.
8. Strain, degrease, and reduce the cooking liquid slightly. Just before serving, moisten each portion with 1-2 tbsp of the liquid.

Chicken Tortilla Soup

Serves:4 Type 2 Prep:10 mins. Cook: 35 mins.

Nutrition per Serving:

191 calories 8 g fat 13 g carbs 19g protein

Ingredients:

- ❖ Extra-virgin olive oil (1 tablespoon)
- ❖ Onion (1, thinly sliced)
- ❖ Garlic clove (1, minced)
- ❖ Jalapeño pepper (1, diced)
- ❖ Chicken breasts (2 boneless, skinless)
- ❖ Chicken broth (9 ½ dl, low-sodium)
- ❖ Roma tomato (1, diced)
- ❖ Salt (½ teaspoon)
- ❖ Corn tortillas (2, cut into thin strips)
- ❖ Non-stick cooking spray
- ❖ Juice of 1 lime
- ❖ Minced fresh coriander, for garnish
- ❖ Cheddar cheese (100g shredded, for garnish)

Directions:

1. Set your oil to heat up over high heat. Add the onion and cook until fragrant and soft (about 3 to 5 minutes).
2. Add the garlic and jalapeño, and cook until fragrant, about 1 minute more.
3. Add in your salt, tomato, broth, and chicken then leave to come to a boil.
4. Once boiling, switch to medium heat and allow to simmer gently for 20 to 25 minutes or as long as it takes for your chicken breasts to fully cook.
5. Remove the chicken from the pot and set aside. Set your broiler to preheat on high.
6. Lightly coat the tortilla strips with cooking spray then toss. Transfer them onto a baking sheet in a single layer and set to broil for 3 to 5 minutes, flipping once, until crisp.
7. When the chicken is cool enough to handle, shred it with two forks and return to the pot.
8. Season the soup with the lime juice. Serve hot, garnished with coriander, cheese, and tortilla strips.

Goat Cheese and Walnut Salad

Serves:3	Type 1	Prep:15 mins.	Cook: 10 mins.

Nutrition per Serving:

460 calories	40 g fat	13 g carbs	17g protein

Ingredients:

- Beet (50g)
- Arugula (85g)
- Bibb lettuce (60g)
- Romaine lettuce (260g)
- Breadcrumbs (90g, dry)
- Dried thyme (1/4 tbs)
- Dried basil (1/4 tbs)
- Black pepper (1/3 tsp)
- Fresh goat's milk cheese (180g, preferably in log shape)
- Walnut pieces (30g)
- Red wine vinaigrette (optional)

Directions:

1. Trim, wash, and dry all the salad greens. Tear the greens into small pieces. Toss well.
2. Mix the herbs, pepper, and crumbs. Slice the cheese into 30 g pieces.
3. In the seasoned crumbs mix, roll the pieces of cheese to coat them
4. Place the cheese on a sheet pan. Bake at the temperate of 220 °C for 10 minutes.
5. At the same time, toast the walnuts in a dry sauté pan or the oven with the cheese.
6. Toss the greens with the vinaigrette and arrange on cold plates. Top each plate of greens with 2 pieces of cheese and sprinkle with walnuts.

Tomato and Kale Soup

Serves:4   Type 2   Prep:10 mins.   Cook: 15 mins.

Nutrition per Serving:

170 calories   5 g fat   31 g carbs   6g protein

Ingredients:

- ❖ Extra-virgin olive oil (1 tbsp.)
- ❖ Onion (1 medium, chopped)
- ❖ Carrots (2, finely chopped)
- ❖ Garlic cloves (3, minced)
- ❖ Vegetable broth (9 ½ dl, low-sodium)
- ❖ Tomatoes (1 can, 800g, crushed)
- ❖ Dried oregano (½ tsp.)
- ❖ Dried basil (¼ tsp.)
- ❖ Baby kale leaves (800g, chopped)
- ❖ Salt (¼ tsp.)

Directions:

1. Over medium heat, set a large pot on with your oil. Add in your carrots and onions.
2. Sauté for 3 to 5 minutes until they begin to soften. Add the garlic and sauté for 30 seconds more, until fragrant.
3. Add the basil, oregano, tomato, and vegetable broth then leave to boil. Reduce the heat to low and simmer for 5 minutes.
4. Using an immersion blender, purée the soup. Add the kale and simmer for 3 more minutes.
5. Season with the salt. Serve immediately.

Panko Coconut Shrimp

Serves:4	Type 2	Prep:12 mins.	Cook: 6-8 mins.

Nutrition per Serving:

181 calories	4 g fat	9 g carbs	28g protein

Ingredients:

- ❖ egg whites (2)
- ❖ water (1 tbsp.)
- ❖ whole-wheat panko breadcrumbs (110 g)
- ❖ coconut flakes (70g unsweetened)
- ❖ turmeric (½ tsp.)
- ❖ ground coriander (½ tsp.)
- ❖ ground cumin (½ tsp.)
- ❖ salt (⅛ tsp.)
- ❖ raw shrimp (450g large, peeled, deveined, and patted dry)
- ❖ Non-stick cooking spray

Directions:

1. Preheat the air fry to 200 ºC. In a shallow dish, beat the egg whites and water until slightly foamy. Set aside.
2. In a separate shallow dish, mix the breadcrumbs, coconut flakes, turmeric, coriander, cumin, and salt, and stir until well combined.
3. Dredge the shrimp in the egg mixture, shaking off any excess, then coat them in the crumb-coconut mixture.
4. Spritz the air fryer basket with non-stick cooking spray and arrange the coated shrimp in the basket.
5. Air fry for 6 to 8 minutes, flipping the shrimp once during cooking, or until the shrimp are golden brown and cooked through.
6. Let the shrimp cool for 5 minutes before serving.

Grilled Spiced Turkey Burger

Serves:3   Type 1   Prep:15 mins.   Cook: 20 mins.

Nutrition per Serving:

250 calories   14 g fat   2 g carbs   27g protein

Ingredients:

- Onion (50g, chopped fine)
- Extra Virgin Olive Oil (1/3 tbsp)
- Turkey (300g, ground)
- Salt (1/3 tbsp)
- Curry powder (1/3 tbsp)
- Lemon zest (2/5 tsp, grated)
- Pepper (1/8 tsp)
- Cinnamon (1/8 tsp)
- Coriander (1/4 tsp, ground)
- Cumin (1/8 tsp, ground)
- Cardamom (1/8 tsp, ground)
- Water (50 ml)
- Tomato Raisin Chutney (as desired)
- Coriander leaves (as desired)

Directions:

1. Cook the onions in the oil until soft. Cool completely.
2. Combine the turkey, onions, spices, water, and salt in a bowl. Toss until mixed.
3. Divide the mixture into portions (as desired). Form each portion into a thick patty.
4. Broil or grill until well done, but do not overcook it, or the burger will dry.
5. Plate the burgers. Place a spoonful of chutney on top of each burger or place it on the side with a small number of greens.
6. You can serve the burger and garnish as a sandwich on whole-grain bread.

Tomato Tea Party Sandwiches

Serves:4   Type 1   Prep:15 mins.   Cook: 0 mins.

Nutrition per Serving:

239 calories   16 g fat   19 g carbs   6g protein

Ingredients:

- Whole wheat bread (4 slices)
- Extra virgin olive oil (4 1/3 tbsp)
- Basil (2 1/8 tbsp., minced)
- Tomato slices (4 thick)
- Ricotta cheese (4 oz)
- Dash of pepper

Directions:

1. Toast bread to your preference. Spread 2 tsp. olive oil on each slice of bread. Add the cheese.
2. Top with tomato, then sprinkle with basil and pepper. Serve with lemon water.

Curried Carrot Soup

Serves:6   Type 2   Prep:10 mins.   Cook: 5 mins.

Nutrition per Serving:

145 calories   11 g fat   13 g carbs   2g protein

Ingredients:

- ❖ Extra-virgin olive oil (1 tbsp.)
- ❖ Onion (1 small, coarsely chopped)
- ❖ Celery stalks (2, coarsely chopped)
- ❖ Curry powder (1½ tsp.)
- ❖ Ground cumin (1 tsp.)
- ❖ Fresh ginger (1 tsp. Minced)
- ❖ Carrots (6 medium, roughly chopped)
- ❖ Vegetable broth (9 ½ dl, low-sodium)
- ❖ Salt (¼ tsp.)
- ❖ Coconut milk (2 ⅓ dl canned)
- ❖ Ground black pepper (¼ tsp.)
- ❖ Fresh cilantro (1 tbsp. Chopped)

Directions:

1. Heat an Instant Pot to high and add the olive oil. Sauté the onion and celery for 2 to 3 minutes.
2. Add the curry powder, cumin, and ginger to the pot and cook until fragrant, about 30 seconds.
3. Add the carrots, vegetable broth, and salt to the pot.
4. Close and seal and set for 5 minutes on high. Allow the pressure to release naturally.
5. In a blender jar, carefully purée the soup in batches and transfer back to the pot.
6. Stir in the coconut milk and pepper, and heat through. Top with the cilantro and serve.

Tuna, Hummus, and Veggie Wraps

Serves:2   Type 2   Prep:2 mins.   Cook: 0 mins.
Nutrition per Serving:
191 calories   5 g fat   15 g carbs   26g protein

Ingredients:
For the hummus:
- ❖ Chickpeas (240g, canned low sodium drained and rinsed)
- ❖ Garlic clove (1)
- ❖ Tahini (2 tbsp.)
- ❖ Extra-virgin olive oil (1 tbsp.)
- ❖ Juice of ½ lemon
- ❖ Salt (¼ tsp.)

- ❖ Water (2 tbsp.)
For the wraps:
- ❖ Chunk light tuna (1 can, 140g in water, drained)
- ❖ Lettuce leaves (4 large)
- ❖ Red bell pepper (1, seeded and cut into strips)
- ❖ Cucumber (1, sliced)

Directions:
To make the hummus:
1. In a blender jar, combine the chickpeas, tahini, olive oil, garlic, lemon juice, salt, and water.
2. Process until smooth. Taste and adjust with additional lemon juice or salt, as needed.

To make the wraps:
1. On each lettuce leaf, spread 1 tablespoon of hummus, and divide the tuna among the leaves.
2. Top each with several strips of red pepper and cucumber slices.
3. Roll up the lettuce leaves, folding in the two shorter sides and rolling away from you, like a burrito. Serve.

Salmon Milano

Serves:6   Type 2   Prep:10 mins.   Cook: 20 mins.
Nutrition per Serving:
445 calories   24 g fat   2 g carbs   55g protein

Ingredients:
- ❖ salmon filet (1.1 kg)
- ❖ tomatoes (2, sliced)
- ❖ margarine (110g)
- ❖ basil pesto (150g)

Directions:
1. Heat the oven to 200 ºC. Line a baking sheet with foil, making sure it covers the sides.
2. Place another large piece of foil onto the baking sheet and place the salmon filet on top of it.
3. Place the pesto and margarine in blender or food processor and pulse until smooth. Spread evenly over salmon. Place tomato slices on top.
4. Wrap the foil around the salmon, tenting around the top to prevent foil from touching the salmon as much as possible.
5. Bake 15 to 25 minutes, or salmon flakes easily with a fork. Serve.

Veggie Shish Kebabs

Serves:3   Type 1   Prep:10 mins.   Cook: 0 mins.
Nutrition per Serving:
349 calories   6 g fat   61 g carbs   15g protein

Ingredients:
- ❖ Skewers (9, wooden)
- ❖ Cherry tomatoes (9)
- ❖ Mozzarella balls (9 low-fat)
- ❖ Basil leaves (9)
- ❖ Olive oil (1 tsp.)
- ❖ Zucchini (3, sliced)
- ❖ Dash of pepper

For Serving:
- ❖ Whole Wheat Bread (6 slices)

Directions:
1. Stab 1 cherry tomato, low-fat mozzarella ball, zucchini, and basil leaf onto each skewer.
2. Place skewers on a plate and drizzle with olive oil. Finish with a sprinkle of pepper.
3. Set your bread to toast. Serve 2 bread slices with 3 kebobs.
4. Enjoy!

Crispy Falafel

Serves:3	Type 1	Prep:20 mins.	Cook: 8 mins.

Nutrition per Serving:

328 calories	11 g fat	48 g carbs	24g protein

Ingredients:

- Chickpeas (240g, drained and rinsed)
- Parsley (90g, chopped with stems removed)
- Coriander (70g, chopped with stems removed)
- Dill (70g, chopped with stems removed)
- Garlic (4 cloves, minced)
- Sesame seeds (1 tbsp., toasted)
- Coriander (½ tbsp.)
- Black pepper (½ tbsp.)
- Cumin (½ tbsp.)
- Baking powder (½ tsp.)
- Cayenne (½ tsp.)
- Olive oil for frying

Directions:

1. Thoroughly dry your chickpeas with a paper towel.
2. Place the parsley, coriander, and dill in a food processor and pulse until it forms mulch.
3. Add in the chickpeas, garlic, coriander, black pepper, cumin, baking powder, and cayenne. Pulse this mixture until smooth and well combined.
4. Transfer the mixture to an airtight container and let it sit in the fridge for about an hour, or until stiff.
5. Remove the mixture from the refrigerator and stir in the baking powder and sesame seeds until well combined.
6. Scoop the mixture into a pan with 8 cm of olive oil over medium heat to create patties.
7. Keep in mind as you create the patties that you are aiming to make 12 with the mixture.
8. Let the falafel patties fry for 1-2 minutes on each side or until golden brown.
9. Once your falafel patties are nicely browned, transfer them to a plate lined with paper towels to finish crisping.
10. Dip, dunk, fill, and enjoy!

Chimichurri Dumplings

Serves:10   Type 2   Prep:20 mins.   Cook: 15 mins.

Nutrition per Serving:

133 calories   1 g fat   26 g carbs   4g protein

Ingredients:

- Water (9 ½ dl)
- Vegetable broth (9 ½ dl, low-sodium)
- Cassava flour (250g)
- All-purpose flour (250g, gluten-free)

- Baking powder (2 tsp.)
- Salt (1 tsp.)
- Fat-free milk (2 ⅓ dl)
- Chimichurri (2 tbsp., bottled)

Directions:

1. In a large pot, bring the water and the broth to a slow boil over medium-high heat.
2. In a large mixing bowl, whisk the cassava flour, all-purpose flour, baking powder, and salt together.
3. In a small bowl, whisk the milk and chimichurri together until combined.
4. Stir the wet ingredients into the dry ingredients a little at a time to create a firm dough.
5. With clean hands, pinch off a small piece of dough. Roll into a ball, and gently flatten in the palm of your hand, forming a disk. Repeat until no dough remains.
6. Carefully drop the dumplings one at a time into the boiling liquid. Cover and simmer for 15 minutes, or until the dumplings are cooked through. You can test by inserting a fork into the dumpling; it should come out clean.
7. Serve warm.

Onion Fried Eggs

Serves:4   Type 1   Prep:15 mins.   Cook: 31 mins.

Nutrition per Serving:

360 calories   27 g fat   10 g carbs   20g protein

Ingredients:

- Eggs (11)
- White mushroom (250g)
- Feta cheese (110g crumbled)
- Sundried tomatoes (110g chopped)
- Onion (2 large, sliced)
- Garlic clove (2, minced)
- Olive oil (2.5 tbsp.)
- Dash of pepper

Directions:

1. Put a pan with the olive oil over medium-low heat. Once the oil is hot, add the onions and mushrooms then stir them into the oil.
2. Allow the onion and mushroom mix to cook for about one hour, or until they become a deep brown colour. Stir them every 5-7 minutes to ensure they cook evenly.
3. After the onions have browned, add the sundried tomatoes and garlic, and let cook for 2 minutes or until fragrant.
4. Once the sundried tomatoes and garlic are fragrant, spread all the ingredients out into an even, thin layer across the pan.
5. Crack the eggs overtop the ingredients already in the pan. Sprinkle your feta cheese and pepper over top of the eggs.
6. Cover the pan with its corresponding lid and let the eggs sit to cook for about 10-12 minutes.
7. Gently shake the pan at 10 minutes to check on the consistency of the egg yolks. Continue to cook until they reach your desired level of doneness.
8. Remove pan from heat and divide the mixture between two plates.
9. Serve, and enjoy!

Coriander Lime Shrimp

Serves:4   Type 2   Prep:15 mins.   Cook: 8 mins.
Nutrition per Serving:
133 calories   4 g fat   1 g carbs   24g protein

Ingredients:
- extra virgin olive oil (1 tsp.)
- garlic clove (½ tsp., minced)
- large shrimp (450g, peeled and deveined)
- fresh coriander 70g, chopped, or more to taste)
- lime (1, zested and juiced)
- salt (¼ tsp.)
- black pepper (⅛ tsp.)

Directions:
1. In a large heavy skillet, heat the olive oil over medium-high heat. Add the minced garlic and cook for 30 seconds until fragrant.
2. Toss in the shrimp and cook for about 5 to 6 minutes, stirring occasionally, or until they turn pink and opaque.
3. Remove from the heat to a bowl. Add the coriander, lime zest and juice, salt, and pepper to the shrimp, and toss to combine.
4. Serve immediately.

Seafood Enchiladas

Serves: 8	Type 2	Prep: 20 mins.	Cook: 1 hr.

Nutrition per Serving:

459 calories	17 g fat	38 g carbs	34g protein

Ingredients:

- Shrimp (570 g medium, raw, peel and devein)
- Halibut (230 g fresh)
- Poblano peppers (2, stemmed, seeded, and diced)
- Red bell pepper (1, diced)
- Onion (1, diced)
- Light sour cream (200g)
- Skim milk (1 ¾ dl)
- Fat cream cheese (110g, reduced, soft)
- Green onions (150g, sliced thin)
- Whole wheat flour tortillas (8, low-carb)
- Water (1.2 L)
- Garlic (2 cloves, diced fine)
- Flour (2 tbsp.)
- Sunflower oil (2 tsp.)
- Salt (¼ tsp.)
- Black pepper (¼ tsp.)
- Non-stick cooking spray

Directions:

1. Rinse shrimp and fish then pat dry with paper towels. Heat oven to 180 °C. Spry a 2.8-L rectangular baking dish with cooking spray.
2. Add water to a large saucepan and bring to boiling over medium-high heat.
3. Add shrimp and cook until shrimp turn pink, 1 to 3 minutes. Drain, rinse with cold water, and chop.
4. Place a steamer insert into a deep skillet with a tight-fitting lid. Add water to just below the insert and bring to a boil.
5. Place fish in the insert, cover and steam 4 to 6 minutes, or until fish flakes easily with a fork.
6. Flake the fish into bite-size pieces and set aside. Heat oil in a large non-stick skillet over medium heat.
7. Add bell pepper, poblanos, and onion. Cook 5 to 10 minutes, or until vegetables are tender.
8. Stir in garlic and 1 minute more. Remove from heat and add shrimp and fish.
9. Wrap tortillas in foil, making sure it's tight, and place in the oven until heated through, about 10 minutes.
10. In a medium bowl, beat cream cheese until smooth. Beat in sour cream, 1/4 teaspoon salt and pepper.
11. Slowly beat in the milk until smooth. Stir 1 ⅛ dl sauce into the fish and shrimp mixture.
12. To assemble, spoon shrimp mixture on one side of the tortillas and roll up.
13. Place, seam side down, in prepare baking dish. Pour remaining sauce over the top.
14. Cover with foil, and bake 35 minutes, or until heated through. Let rest 5 minutes before serving. Garnish with chopped green onions.

Pan Seared Trout and Salsa

Serves:6	Type 2	Prep:5 mins.	Cook: 10 mins.

Nutrition per Serving:

321 calories	21 g fat	2 g carbs	30g protein

Ingredients:
- Trout filets (6)
- Lemon slices (6)
- Olive oil (4 tbsp.)
- Salt (¾ tsp.)
- Pepper (½ tsp.)

Italian Salsa:
- Plum tomatoes (4, diced)
- Red onion (½, diced fine)
- Fresh parsley (2 tbsp., diced)
- Kalamata olives (12, pitted and chopped)
- Garlic (2 cloves, diced fine)
- Balsamic vinegar (1 tbsp.)
- Olive oil (1 tbsp.)
- Capers (2 tsp., drained)
- Salt (¼ tsp.)
- Pepper (¼ tsp.)

Directions:
1. Sprinkle filets with salt and pepper. Heat oil in a large skillet, preferably non-stick, on medium heat.
2. Cook trout, 3 filets at a time, 2 to 3 minutes per side, or fish flakes easily with a fork. Repeat with remaining filets.
3. Meanwhile, combine the ingredients for the salsa in a small bowl. Serve the trout topped with salsa and a slice of lemon.

Paella

Serves:6   Type 2   Prep:25 mins.   Cook: 35 mins.

Nutrition per Serving:

424 calories   18 g fat   21 g carbs   46g protein

Ingredients:

- ❖ Chicken thighs (450g, skinless and boneless)
- ❖ Shrimp (450g medium, raw, peel and devein)
- ❖ Mussels (1 dozen, cleaned)
- ❖ Chorizo sausages (2, cut into pieces)
- ❖ Head cauliflower (1 medium, grated)
- ❖ Yellow onion (1, diced fine)
- ❖ Green bell pepper (1, sliced into strips)
- ❖ Frozen peas (140g)
- ❖ Tomatoes (1 can, 430g, diced, drain well)
- ❖ Extra-virgin olive oil (2 tbsp.)
- ❖ Garlic (2 tsp., diced fine
- ❖ Salt (2 tsp.)
- ❖ Saffron (1 tsp.)
- ❖ Pepper (½ tsp.)
- ❖ Paprika (¼ tsp.)
- ❖ Non-stick cooking spray

Directions:

1. Heat the oven to broil. Spray a baking dish with cooking spray.
2. Sprinkle salt and pepper on both sides of the chicken and place in baking dish.
3. Bake, about 4 minutes per side, until no longer pink in the middle. Let cool completely.
4. Heat 1 tablespoon of the oil in a medium skillet over medium heat. Add onion, pepper, and garlic.
5. Cook, about 4 to 5 minutes, stirring frequently, until peppers start to get soft. Transfer to a bowl.
6. Add chorizo to the skillet and cook 2 minutes, stirring frequently. Drain off the fat and add to the vegetables.
7. Once the chicken has cooled, cut into small pieces and add it to the vegetables.
8. In a large saucepot, over medium heat, add the remaining oil. Once it is hot, add the cauliflower and seasonings. Cook 8 to 10 minutes, until cauliflower is almost tender, stirring frequently.
9. Add the mussels and shrimp and cook until mussels open, and shrimp start to turn pink.
10. Add the mixture in the bowl with the tomatoes and peas and stir to combine everything together.
11. Cook another 5 minutes until everything is heated through and all of the mussels have opened. Serve.

Monterey Crab Quiche

Serves:16   Type 2   Prep:20 mins.   Cook: 45 mins.

Nutrition per Serving:

252 calories   13 g fat   22 g carbs   14g protein

Ingredients:

- Lump crab meat (230g)
- Egg whites (8, dived)
- Eggs (4)
- Cottage cheese (440g, low fat)
- Monterey jack cheese (470g, grated)
- Onion (110g, diced)
- Margarine (1 tbsp.)
- Pie crusts (2, 23-cm)
- Green chilies (2 cans, 110 g each, chopped)
- Flour (70g)
- Garlic (2 cloves, diced fine)
- Baking powder (¾ tsp.)
- Salt (¼ tsp.)

Directions:

1. Heat oven to 200 °C.
2. Melt margarine in a small skillet over medium-low heat. Add onion and cook until tender. Add garlic and cook 1 minute more.
3. In a large bowl, combine 6 egg whites, eggs, cottage cheese, cheese, chilies, crab, flour, baking powder, onion mixture, and salt.
4. In a separate large bowl, beat remaining egg whites until stiff peaks form. Fold into crab mixture. Pour into pie crusts.
5. Bake 10 minutes, reduce heat to 180 °C, and bake 30 minutes. Sprinkle with remaining cheese and bake 5 minutes more, or a knife inserted in centres comes out clean.
6. Let cool 10 minutes before slicing and serving.

Veggie Fajitas with Guacamole

Serves:4   Type 2   Prep:10 mins.   Cook: 15 mins.

Nutrition per Serving:

270 calories   15 g fat   30 g carbs   8g protein

Ingredients:

For the Guacamole:
- Avocados (2 small, pitted and peeled)
- Lime juice (1 tsp., freshly squeezed)
- Salt (¼ tsp.)
- Cherry tomatoes (9, halved)

For the Fajitas:
- Red bell pepper (1)
- Green bell pepper (1)
- White onion (1 small)
- Avocado oil cooking spray
- Black beans (230g, canned low-sodium, drained and rinsed)
- Ground cumin (½ tsp.)
- Chili powder (¼ tsp.)
- Garlic powder (¼ tsp.)
- Yellow corn tortillas (4, 15-cm in size)

Directions:

To Make the Guacamole:
1. In a medium bowl, use a fork to mash the avocados with the lime juice and salt.
2. Gently stir in the cherry tomatoes.

To Make the Fajitas:
1. Heat a large skillet over medium heat. When hot, coat the cooking surface with cooking spray. Put the peppers, onion, and beans into the skillet.
2. Add the cumin, chili powder, and garlic powder, and stir. Cover and cook for 15 minutes, stirring halfway through.
3. Divide the fajita mixture equally between the tortillas, and top with guacamole and any preferred garnishes.

Spaghetti Squash and Chickpea Bolognese

Serves:4	Type 2	Prep:5 mins.	Cook: 25 mins.

Nutrition per Serving:

276 calories	7 g fat	42 g carbs	14g protein

Ingredients:

- ❖ Spaghetti squash (650g)
- ❖ Ground cumin (½ tsp.)
- ❖ Spaghetti sauce (250 ml, sugar-free)
- ❖ Chickpeas (1 can, 425 g, low-sodium, drained and rinsed)
- ❖ Extra-firm tofu (170 g)

Directions:

1. Preheat the oven to 200 °C. Cut the squash in half lengthwise. Scoop out the seeds and discard.
2. Season both halves of the squash with the cumin and place them on a baking sheet cut side down. Roast for 25 minutes.
3. Meanwhile, heat a medium saucepan over low heat, and pour in the spaghetti sauce and chickpeas.
4. Press the tofu between two layers of paper towels, and gently squeeze out any excess water.
5. Crumble the tofu into the sauce and cook for 15 minutes.
6. Remove the squash from the oven, and comb through the flesh of each half with a fork to make thin strands.
7. Divide the "spaghetti" into four portions and top each portion with one-quarter of the sauce.

Tomato Tuna Melts

Serves:2   Type 2   Prep:5 mins.   Cook: 5 mins.

Nutrition per Serving:

243 calories   10 g fat   7 g carbs   30g protein

Ingredients:

- Chunk light tuna (1 can, 140g in water, drained)
- Greek yogurt (2 tbsp., plain non-fat)
- Lemon juice (2 tsp., freshly squeezed)
- Celery (2 tbsp., finely chopped)
- Red onion (1 tbsp., finely chopped)
- Pinch cayenne pepper
- 2-cm-thick rounds
- Cheddar cheese (100g, shredded)

Directions:

1. Preheat the broiler to high.
2. In a medium bowl, combine the tuna, yogurt, lemon juice, celery, red onion, and cayenne pepper. Stir well.
3. Arrange the tomato slices on a baking sheet. Top each with some tuna salad and cheddar cheese.
4. Broil for 3 to 4 minutes until the cheese is melted and bubbly. Serve.

Ras-El-Hanout Chicken Traybake

Serves:4	Type 2	Prep:20 mins.	Cook: 50 mins.

Nutrition per Serving:

361 calories	6 g fat	30 g carbs	44g protein

Ingredients:

- Chicken breast fillets (170g)
- Sweet potatoes (400g, peeled and cubed)
- Garlic cloves (3)
- Carrots (400g, peeled and cubed)
- Olive oil (1 tbsp)
- Thyme (1 sprigs, handful)
- Red onion (1, large, sliced in wedges)
- Ras-el-hanout spice mix (2 tsp)
- Lemon (1, quartered)
- Coriander (1, handful, finely chopped)
- Salt and black pepper
- Yoghurt (4 tbsp low-fat natural, to serve)

Directions:

1. Set the oven temperature to 90 °C. In a roasting pan, combine the carrots and sweet potatoes. Season with salt and pepper and drizzle with oil.
2. Let it roast for 10 minutes. Stir in the onion and garlic. Continue to roast for 20 more minutes.
3. Cook the chicken breasts in a roasting pan with the lemon quarters in a single layer. Add ras-el-hanout, thyme, and olive oil to everything.
4. The chicken should be cooked through after another 15-20 minutes of roasting. Add the coriander and stir well.
5. Slice the lemon and divide chicken between four plates. Squeeze lemon juice over each and serve with yoghurt.

Light Lemony Pasta and Spinach Bake

Serves:4	Type 2	Prep:15 mins.	Cook: mins.

Nutrition per Serving:

459 calories	11 g fat	63 g carbs	24g protein

Ingredients:

- Olive oil (2 tsp)
- Macaroni (300g, dried)
- Garlic clove (1, sliced thinly)
- Broccoli (200g, florets)
- Spring onions (2, thinly sliced)
- Baby spinach (100g, leaves)
- Flour (1 tbsp, plain)
- Bay leaves (2)
- Skimmed milk (300 ml)
- Zest of 1 lemon
- Wholegrain mustard (1 tsp)
- Salt and black pepper
- Parmesan cheese (100g, finely grated)

Salad:

- Olive oil (1 tsp)
- Lemon juice, a squeeze
- Mixed salad

Directions:

1. Prepare the oven by preheating it to 200 °C. Cook the macaroni for 6 minutes in boiling water.
2. Stir in your broccoli then cook for another two minutes. Switch off the heat, add in your spinach then allow to stand covered for another 2 minutes. Drain then set aside
3. Set your oil to get hot in a heavy-set frying pan. Add in your spring onions and cook until fragrant (2 minutes). Next, stir in your garlic the garlic and continue to stir while cooking for 2 more minutes.
4. Stir in your flour and cook until incorporated (about 2 minutes). Pour in your milk in a slow stream, season then add in your bay leaves.
5. Allow to simmer until thickened (about 2-3 minutes). Discard your bay leaves.
6. Stir in your lemon zest, ¾ of your parmesan and mustard, then season to taste.
7. Transfer your broccoli and pasta to a shallow baking dish. Top with your sauce and mix to combine.
8. Add the rest of your cheese evenly on top of your pasta and broccoli then set to bake until beautifully melted (about 15-20 minutes).
9. Serve with your salad. Enjoy!

Butter-Lemon Grilled Cod on Asparagus

Serves:4   Type 2   Prep:5 mins.   Cook: 9-12 mins.

Nutrition per Serving:

158 calories   6 g fat   6 g carbs   23g protein

Ingredients:

- ❖ Asparagus spears (450g, ends trimmed)
- ❖ Cooking spray
- ❖ Cod fillets (4 (110g), rinsed and patted dry)
- ❖ Black pepper (¼ tsp., optional)
- ❖ Light butter (60g, with canola oil)
- ❖ Juice and zest of 1 medium lemon
- ❖ Salt (¼ tsp., optional)

Directions:

1. Heat a grill pan over medium-high heat.
2. Spray the asparagus spears with cooking spray. Cook the asparagus for 6 to 8 minutes until fork-tender, flipping occasionally.
3. Transfer to a large platter and keep warm.
4. Spray both sides of fillets with cooking spray. Season with ¼ teaspoon black pepper, if needed.
5. Add the fillets to the pan and sear each side for 3 minutes until opaque.
6. Meantime, in a small bowl, whisk together the light butter, lemon zest, and ¼ teaspoon salt (if desired).
7. Spoon and spread the mixture all over the asparagus. Place the fish on top and squeeze the lemon juice over the fish.
8. Serve immediately.

Mediterranean Sushi

Serves:4   Type 1   Prep:15 mins.   Cook: 0 mins.

Nutrition per Serving:

408 calories   20 g fat   36 g carbs   24g protein

Ingredients:

- Cucumber (12 large)
- Tomatoes (250g, sun-dried, diced)
- Hummus (550g)
- Feta cheese (400g, low-fat, crumbled)
- Garlic (24 cloves, minced)
- Dash pepper

Directions:

1. Using a vegetable sheer, peel the outside skin off the cucumber. Create 6 thin pieces by slicing lengthwise.
2. Lay cucumber slices out side-by-side on a cutting board. Layer about 1 ½ teaspoon of hummus over each cucumber slice.
3. Top each slice with 1 ½ teaspoon sun-dried tomatoes and low-fat feta cheese. Sprinkle with pepper.
4. Pick up the end of a cucumber slice that is closest to you and begin to roll so that ingredients are on the inside.
5. Ensure not to roll too tight or the filling will squish out. Secure each roll with a toothpick.
6. Repeat steps 8-9 for the remaining slices of cucumber. Plate and enjoy it!

Pan- Smoked Trout Fillet with Pepper Salad

| Serves:3 | Type 1 | Prep:10 mins. | Cook: 12 mins. |

Nutrition per Serving:

| 370 calories | 25 g fat | 9 g carbs | 29 g protein |

Ingredients:

- ❖ Trout fillet (300g)
- ❖ Extra Virgin Olive Oil (2 tbsp)
- ❖ Ground coriander (1/4 tsp)
- ❖ Ground cumin (1/4 tsp)
- ❖ Ground cloves (1/8 tsp)
- ❖ Ground fennel (1/4 tsp)
- ❖ Black pepper (1/4 tsp)
- ❖ Salt (1/4 tsp)
- ❖ Roasted pepper salad (340g)

Directions:

1. Cut the trout fillets into 4 oz portions. Brush the trout lightly with oil.
2. Sprinkle your spices and salt lightly on top of your fish in an even layer.
3. Set up a smoke roasting system. Set your sawdust or wood chips to get hot in a pan on the stove until it begins to smoke.
4. Lay the trout fillets on the rack, cover, and turn the heat to medium-low. Set to smoke for about 2 minutes.
5. Remove from smoke and set to bake in a preheated 200 °C oven. Roast until the fish is fully cooked through (about 8-10 minutes).
6. Serves immediately with pepper salad.

Pan-Smoked Spiced Chicken Breasts with Fruit Salsa

Serves: 3   Type 1   Prep: 15 mins.   Cook: 20 mins.

Nutrition per Serving:

200 calories   6 g fat   7 g carbs   29g protein

Ingredients:

- Paprika (1/2 tbsp)
- Ground cumin (½ tsp)
- Dried thyme (1/4 tsp)
- Ground coriander (½ tsp)
- Salt (½ tsp)
- Pepper (1/4 tsp)
- Chicken breasts (3, boneless and skinless, 140g each)
- Extra Virgin Olive Oil (as needed)
- Wheatberries (280g, with Pecans and Poblanos)
- Fruit Salsa (170g)
- Coriander sprigs (as needed, for garnish, optional)

Directions:

1. Combine the cumin, paprika, thyme, salt, pepper, and coriander. Coat the breast with the spice mixture.
2. Brush with oil lightly. Allow marinating, refrigerated, 3-4 hours.
3. Set up a smoke-roasting system. Heat the pan of sawdust or wood chips on the stovetop until smoke appears.
4. Place the chicken on a rack and cover it. Turn the heat to medium. Smoke roast 10 minutes.
5. Transfer the pan to an oven preheated to 204 C and roast for another 10 minutes.
6. For each portion, place an 85 g portion of wheatberries on the centre of a plate.
7. Slice a chicken breast on the diagonal and arrange the slices, overlapping, on top of the wheatberries.
8. Spoon 56 g salsa next to the chicken and wheatberries. Garnish with coriander.

Baked Chicken with Brown Rice & Veggies

Serves:3	Type 1	Prep:10 mins.	Cook: 1 hr.

Nutrition per Serving:

532 calories	31 g fat	23 g carbs	40g protein

Ingredients:

- ❖ Whole wheat flour (30g)
- ❖ Salt (1½ tsp)
- ❖ White pepper (1/8 tsp)
- ❖ Paprika (1/4 tsp)
- ❖ Dried thyme (1/8 tsp)
- ❖ Roma Tomato (3, large, sliced)
- ❖ Broccoli (85g., cut in florets)
- ❖ Parsley (1 bunch, stems removed)
- ❖ Fryer chicken parts (850g)
- ❖ Extra Virgin Olive Oil (85g)
- ❖ Brown rice (230g)
- ❖ Water (4 ¾ dl)

Directions:

1. Combine the flour and seasonings in a pan. Dry the chicken pieces with paper towels if they are wet. Dredge in the seasoned flour.
2. Place the chicken in the Extra Virgin Olive Oil so that it is coated fully. Let excess drip off.
3. Place the chicken on a sheet pan, with the skin side up. If using both dark and light meat parts, place them on separate pans. Add your broccoli in around your chicken.
4. Bake the chicken at 204 C until done, about 45 mins.
5. Rinse your brown rice and set it on high heat with your ½ tsp salt and water. Cover and allow to come to a boil.
6. Switch to a low heat to simmer for another 45 minutes. Switch off your heat and leave covered for about 10 minutes.
7. When ready to serve. Split your rice, chicken, and tomatoes evenly and store or enjoy.

Fresh Rosemary Trout

| Serves:2 | Type 2 | Prep:5 mins. | Cook: 8 mins. |

Nutrition per Serving:

| 180 calories | 9 g fat | 0 g carbs | 24g protein |

Ingredients:

- Rosemary sprigs (4 to 6 fresh)
- Trout fillets (220g, rinsed and patted dry)
- Olive oil (½ tsp.)
- Salt (⅛ tsp.)
- Pepper (⅛ tsp.)
- Fresh lemon juice (1 tsp.)

Directions:

1. Preheat the oven to 180°C.
2. Put the rosemary sprigs in a small baking pan in a single row. Spread the fillets on the top of the rosemary sprigs.
3. Brush both sides of each piece of fish with the olive oil. Sprinkle with the salt, pepper, and lemon juice.
4. Bake in the preheated oven for 7 to 8 minutes, or until the fish is opaque and flakes easily.
5. Divide the fillets between two plates and serve hot.

Tomato Basil Stuffed Peppers

Serves:6   Type 1   Prep:15 mins.   Cook: 71 mins.

Nutrition per Serving:

349 calories   13 g fat   46 g carbs   14g protein

Ingredients:

- Tofu (450g, crumbled)
- Bell peppers (4, the colour of your preference)
- Tomato sauce (1 can)
- Brown rice (350g, cooked)
- Heavy cream (¾ dl)
- Basil (70g, chopped)
- Feta cheese (170g)
- Garlic cloves (3, minced)
- Onion (½, diced)
- Olive oil (1 tbsp.)
- Dash of pepper

Directions:

1. Preheat oven to 200 ºC.
2. Slice the tops off the peppers and scoop out their insides. Discard them and set the peppers aside.
3. Put the tofu in a bowl and fold the pepper into it until evenly distributed.
4. Place the pan with the olive oil over medium heat.
5. When the oil is hot, add the onion and let it cook for about 5 minutes or until translucent.
6. Once the onion is translucent, add 2 garlic cloves and cook for 1 minute or until fragrant.
7. As soon as the garlic is fragrant, add the seasoned the crumbled tofu and let it cook for 10-15 minutes or until cooked through.
8. While the tofu cooks, combine the heavy cream, and the left-over garlic clove and mix.
9. Transfer this mixture to a saucepan. Place the saucepan on low heat and stir in some basil, leaving a little bit to garnish your peppers later.
10. Stir the brown rice and feta cheese into the tofu mixture until well combined.
11. Pour half of the tomato sauce mixture into the pan and stir again until well combined. Remove from heat.
12. Line your bell peppers close together and divide the frying pan mixture between them, pouring it into each pepper until full.
13. Spoon about 2 teaspoons of the remaining cream sauce into each pepper.
14. Transfer the peppers to a baking pan and pour the remainder of the tomato sauce into the bottom of the pan.
15. Place the tops back on the peppers and stick them in the oven for 20 minutes.
16. Remove the baking pan from the oven, cover the peppers with aluminium foil.
17. Place the baking pan back in the oven and cook for an additional 30 minutes.
18. Remove the baking pan from the oven, discard the aluminium foil, and garnish with the remaining basil.
19. Place 2 peppers on each plate, serve with a glass of wine, and enjoy!

Chicken Paillard with Grilled Vegetables

| Serves:4 | Type 1 | Prep:12 mins. | Cook: 20 mins. |

Nutrition per Serving:

| 250 calories | 11 g fat | 1 g carbs | 34g protein |

Ingredients:

- ❖ Chicken breast (4 boneless, skinless about 170g each)
- ❖ Garlic cloves (1, chopped)
- ❖ Fresh rosemary (1/3 tbsp, chopped)
- ❖ Salt (1/4 tsp)

- ❖ Pepper (1/8 tsp)
- ❖ Lemon juice (30 ml)
- ❖ Olive oil (30 ml)
- ❖ Grilled vegetable medley (as desired)
- ❖ Fresh rosemary (4 sprigs)

Directions:
1. Place your chicken breasts between 2 sheets of plastic film. With a meat mallet, carefully pound to about 6 mm.
2. Combine the rosemary, garlic, pepper, and salt. Rub the flattened chicken on both sides with the mixture.
3. Sprinkle both sides with the lemon juice, then with the olive oil. Let marinate 2-4 hours in the refrigerator.
4. Preheat a grill or broiler to very hot. Place the chicken breasts and veggies on the grill or under your broiler, skin side (that is, the side that had the skin on) down, and grill until about one-fourth has done.
5. Rotate on the grill to mark. Continue to cook until about half has done. Turnover and continue to grill until just cooked through.
6. Plate and serve. Garnish with a sprig of rosemary.

Lemon Parsley White Fish Fillets

Serves:4   Type 2   Prep:10 mins.   Cook: 10 mins.

Nutrition per Serving:

283 calories   17 g fat   1 g carbs   33g protein

Ingredients:
- Lean white fish fillets (4, rinsed and patted dry)
- Cooking spray
- Paprika (to taste)
- Salt and pepper (to taste)
- Parsley (2 tbsp., finely chopped)
- Lemon zest (½ tsp.)
- Extra virgin olive oil (60 ml)
- Dried dill (¼ tsp.)
- Lemon (1 medium, halved)

Directions:
1. Preheat the oven to 200 ºC. Line a baking sheet with aluminum foil and spray with cooking spray.
2. Place the fillets on the foil and scatter with the paprika. Season as desired.
3. Bake in the preheated oven for 10 minutes, or until the flesh flakes easily with a fork.
4. Meanwhile, stir together the parsley, lemon zest, olive oil, and dill in a small bowl.
5. Remove the fish from the oven to four plates. Squeeze the lemon juice over the fish and serve topped with the parsley mixture.

Chunky Vegetable Soup

Serves: 3   Type 1   Prep: 15 mins.   Cook: 20 mins.

Nutrition per Serving:

540 calories   10 g fat   88 g carbs   27g protein

Ingredients:

- Olive oil (1¼ tbsp)
- Onion (2 chopped)
- Vegetable broth (1.7 L)
- Tomatoes (650g canned)
- Oregano (2 tsp)
- Basil (2 tsp dried)
- Parsley (2 tbsp dried)
- Bay leaves (7)
- Carrots (4 chopped)
- Butternut squash (4 diced)
- Celery stalks (4, diced)
- Kidney beans (4 cans, drained and rinsed)
- Dash of pepper
- Dash of Italian seasoning

Directions:

1. Heat oil in a large pot. Add onions and brown.
2. Add broth, tomatoes, basil, oregano, parsley, butternut squash, celery, carrots, and boil the mixture.
3. Turn the heat down and simmer for 15 minutes until vegetables are tender.
4. Add the beans and cook until heated through about another 3 minutes. Season with salt and pepper.
5. Serve hot with rice or bread.

Cheesy Eggplant Sandwiches

Serves:4   Type 1   Prep:15 mins.   Cook: 12 mins.

Nutrition per Serving:

398 calories   19 g fat   49 g carbs   15g protein

Ingredients:

- ❖ Olive oil (1¼ tbsp)
- ❖ Onion (2 chopped)
- ❖ Vegetable broth (1.7 L)
- ❖ Tomatoes (650g, canned)
- ❖ Oregano (2 tsp)
- ❖ Basil (2 tsp dried)
- ❖ Parsley (2 tbsp dried)
- ❖ Bay leaves (7)

- ❖ Carrots (4 chopped)
- ❖ Butternut squash (4 diced)
- ❖ Celery stalks (4, diced)
- ❖ Kidney beans (4 cans, drained and rinsed)
- ❖ Dash of pepper
- ❖ Dash of Italian seasoning

Directions:

1. Heat oil in a large pot. Add onions and brown.
2. Add broth, tomatoes, basil, oregano, parsley, butternut squash, celery, carrots, and boil the mixture.
3. Turn the heat down and simmer for 15 minutes until vegetables are tender.
4. Add the beans and cook until heated through about another 3 minutes. Season with salt and pepper.
5. Serve hot with rice or bread.

Cod Fillet with Quinoa and Asparagus

Serves:4   Type 2   Prep:5 mins.   Cook: 15 mins.

Nutrition per Serving:

258 calories   8 g fat   23 g carbs   25g protein

Ingredients:

- ❖ Quinoa (110g, uncooked)
- ❖ Cod fillets (4, 120g each)
- ❖ Garlic powder (½ tsp., divided)
- ❖ Salt (¼ tsp.)
- ❖ Ground black pepper (¼ tsp.)
- ❖ Asparagus spears (24, cut the bottom 4 cm off)
- ❖ Avocado oil (1 tbsp.)
- ❖ Half-and-half (220g)

Directions:

1. Put the quinoa in a pot of salted water. Bring to a boil.
2. Reduce the heat to low and simmer for 15 minutes or until the quinoa is soft and has a white "tail".
3. Cover and turn off the heat. Let sit for 5 minutes. On a clean work surface, rub the cod fillets with ¼ teaspoon of garlic powder, salt, and pepper.
4. Heat the avocado oil in a non-stick skillet over medium-low heat.
5. Add the cod fillets and asparagus in the skillet and cook for 8 minutes or until they are tender.
6. Flip the cod and shake the skillet halfway through the cooking time.
7. Pour the half-and-half in the skillet, and sprinkle with remaining garlic powder. Turn up the heat to high and simmer for 2 minutes until creamy.
8. Divide the quinoa, cod fillets, and asparagus in four bowls and serve warm.

Tartar Tuna Patties

Serves:4   Type 2   Prep:5 mins.   Cook: 8-10 mins.

Nutrition per Serving:

529 calories   34 g fat   18 g carbs   35g protein

Ingredients:

- ❖ Tuna (450g canned, drained)
- ❖ Whole-wheat breadcrumbs (200g)
- ❖ Eggs (2 large, lightly beaten)
- ❖ Juice and zest of 1 lemon
- ❖ Onion (½, grated)
- ❖ Fresh dill (1 tbsp. Chopped)
- ❖ Extra-virgin olive oil (3 tbsp.)
- ❖ Tartar sauce (110g, for topping)

Directions:

1. Mix together the tuna with the breadcrumbs, beaten eggs, lemon juice and zest, onion, and dill in a large bowl, and stir until well incorporated.
2. Scoop out the tuna mixture and shape into 4 equal-sized patties with your hands.
3. Transfer the patties to a plate and chill in the refrigerator for 10 minutes.
4. Once chilled, heat the olive oil in a large skillet, preferably non-stick, on medium heat.
5. Add the patties to the skillet and cook each side for 4 to 5 minutes, or until nicely browned on both sides.
6. Remove the patties from the heat and top with the tartar sauce.

Broiled Teriyaki Salmon

Serves:4   Type 2   Prep:5 mins.   Cook: 3-5 mins.

Nutrition per Serving:

201 calories   7 g fat   9 g carbs   24g protein

Ingredients:

- Soy sauce (80 ml low-sodium)
- Pineapple juice (80 ml)
- Water (⅔ dl)
- Rice vinegar (2 tbsp.)
- Garlic clove (1, minced)
- Honey (1 tbsp.)
- Fresh ginger (1 tsp. Peeled and grated)
- Pinch red pepper flakes
- Salmon fillet (450 g, cut into 4 pieces)

Directions:

1. Preheat the oven broiler on high.
2. Stir together the soy sauce, pineapple juice, water, vinegar, garlic, honey, ginger, and red pepper flakes in a small bowl.
3. Marinate the fillets (flesh-side down) in the sauce for about 5 minutes.
4. Transfer the fillets (flesh-side up) to a rimmed baking sheet and brush them generously with any leftover sauce.
5. Broil the fish until it flakes apart easily and reaches an internal temperature of 60 ℃, about 3 to 5 minutes.
6. Let the fish cool for 5 minutes before serving.

Marinated Grilled Salmon with Lemongrass

Serves:4   Type 2   Prep:10mins.   Cook: 8-12 mins.

Nutrition per Serving:

223 calories   12 g fat   2 g carbs   26g protein

Ingredients:

- Olive oil (1 tbsp.)
- Fresh ginger (1 tbsp., grated)
- Hot chili pepper (1 small)
- Lemongrass (1 tbsp., minced)

- Soy sauce (2 tbsp., low-sodium)
- Honey (1 tbsp.)
- Salmon fillets (4,120 g skinless)

Directions:

1. Except for the salmon, stir together all the ingredients in a medium bowl. Brush the salmon fillets generously with the marinade and place in the fridge to marinate for 30 minutes.
2. Preheat the grill to medium heat.
3. Discard the marinade and transfer the salmon to the preheated grill.
4. Grill each side for 4 to 6 minutes, or until the fish is almost completely cooked through at the thickest part. Serve hot.

Grilled Shrimp Skewers

Serves:4	Type 2	Prep:10 mins.	Cook: 12 mins.

Nutrition per Serving:

122 calories	1 g fat	3 g carbs	26g protein

Ingredients:

- ❖ Shrimp (450 g, shelled and deveined)
- ❖ Greek yogurt (110g, plain)
- ❖ Chili paste (½ tbsp.)
- ❖ Lime juice (½ tbsp.)

- ❖ Chopped green onions, for garnish
- ❖ Special Equipment:
- ❖ Wooden skewers, soaked in water for at least 30 minutes

Directions:

1. Thread the shrimp onto skewers, piercing once near the tail and once near the head.
2. You can place about 5 shrimps on each skewer. Preheat the grill to medium.
3. Place the shrimp skewers on the grill and cook for about 6 minutes, flipping the shrimp halfway through, or until the shrimp are totally pink and opaque.
4. Meanwhile, make the yogurt and chili sauce: In a small bowl, stir together the yogurt, chili paste, and lime juice.
5. Transfer the shrimp skewers to a large plate. Scatter the green onions on top for garnish and serve with the yogurt and chili sauce on the side.

Black Bean Cake with Salsa

Serves:20	Type 1	Prep:15 mins.	Cook: 20 mins.

Nutrition per Serving:

260 calories	12 g fat	30 g carbs	9g protein

Ingredients:
- ❖ Olive oil (30 ml)
- ❖ Onion (450g, cut brunoised)
- ❖ Garlic (2-4 cloves, chopped)
- ❖ Jalapenos (seeded and brunoised)
- ❖ Ground cumin (2 tsp)

- ❖ Black beans (910 g, cooked)
- ❖ Oregano (1 tsp, dried)
- ❖ Salt (to taste)
- ❖ Pepper (to taste)
- ❖ Salsa cruda (450 ml)

Directions:
1. Heat the olive oil in a sauté pan over low heat. Add the garlic and onions, cook until soft. Do not brown.
2. Add the ground cumin and jalapeno. Cook for a few more minutes. Add the oregano and beans. Cook until they are heated through.
3. Place the mixture in a food processor and blend in a puree. The mixture should be thick to hold its shape. If the mixture becomes too dry, moisten with a little water.
4. Adjust the seasoning with salt and pepper if needed. Divide the mixture into 50 g portions. Form into small, flat cakes.
5. Brown the cakes lightly on both sides in hot olive oil in a sauté pan. They will be exceptionally soft; handle carefully.
6. Serve 2 cakes per portion with salsa.

Pickled Apple

Serves: 12 oz	Type 2	Prep: 10 mins.	Cook: 0 mins.

Nutrition per Serving:

50 calories	0 g fat	12 g carbs	0 g protein

Ingredients:
- ❖ Water (1 ⅛ dl)
- ❖ Honey (100g)
- ❖ Cider vinegar (1 ⅛ dl)

Sachet:
- ❖ Peppercorns (3-4)
- ❖ Mustard seed (1/4 tsp)
- ❖ Coriander seed (1/4 tsp)
- ❖ Salt (1/4 tsp)
- ❖ Granny smith apple (2, peeled, cored, and cut into small dice)
- ❖ Italian parsley (1 tbsp, cut chiffonade)

Directions:
1. Combine the water, honey, vinegar, sachet, and sat in a saucepan. Bring to a boil.
2. Pour the liquid and the sachet over the apples in a nonreactive container.
3. Let it be refrigerated for 3-4 hours or overnight.
4. Drain the apples before serving and toss with the parsley.

Baked Clams Oreganata

Serves:10   Type 1   Prep:30 mins.   Cook: 15 mins.

Nutrition per Serving:

180 calories   8 g fat   16 g carbs   10g protein

Ingredients:

- Cherrystone clams (30, removed from shell and juices reserved)
- Olive oil (60 ml)
- Onions (30g, chopped fine)
- Garlic (1 tsp, finely chopped)
- Lemon juice (30 ml)
- Fresh breadcrumbs (280 g)
- Parsley (1 tbsp, chopped)
- Oregano (3/4 tsp, dried)
- White pepper (1/8 tsp)
- Parmesan cheese (80g)
- Paprika (as needed)
- Lemon wedges (10)

Directions:

1. Chop the clams into small pieces. Heat the oil in a sauté pan. Add the onion and garlic. Sauté about 1 minute, but do not brown.
2. Use half of the clam juice, then reduce it over high heat by three-fourths.
3. Remove from the heat and add the crumbs, parsley, lemon juice, white pepper, and oregano. Mix gently to avoid making the crumbs pasty.
4. If necessary, adjust the seasonings. Once the mixture has cooled. Mix in the chopped clams.
5. Place the mixture in the 30 clamshells. Sprinkle with paprika and parmesan cheese.
6. Transfer to a sheet pan and refrigerate until needed.
7. For each order, bake 3 clams in a hot oven (232 C) until they are hot and the top brown.
8. Garnish with a lemon wedge.

Tuna Tartare

Serves:8   Type 1   Prep:15 mins.   Cook: 0 mins.

Nutrition per Serving:

200 calories   12 g fat   2 g carbs   21g protein

Ingredients:

- Sashimi quality tuna (200g, well-trimmed)
- Shallots (50g minced)
- Parsley (2 tbsp, chopped)
- Fresh tarragon (2 tbsp, chopped)
- Lime juice (2 tbsp)
- Dijon-style mustard (30 ml)
- Olive oil (70 ml)
- Salt (to taste)
- White pepper (to taste)

Directions:

1. Use a knife to mince the tuna.
2. Mixed the rest of the ingredients with the chopped tuna before serving. Season to taste with pepper and salt.

Cod Cakes

Serves:12   Type 1   Prep:40 mins.   Cook: 20 mins.

Nutrition per Serving:

280 calories   6 g fat   33 g carbs   23g protein

Ingredients:

- Cod (340g, cooked)
- Turnips puree (340g)
- Whole eggs (70g, beaten)
- Egg yolk (1 yolk, beaten)
- Salt (to taste)
- White pepper (to taste)
- Ground ginger (pinch)
- Standard Breading Procedure:
- Whole wheat flour (as needed)
- Egg wash (as needed)
- Breadcrumbs (as needed)
- Tomatoes sauce (as desired)

Directions:

1. Flake the fish until it is well shredded. Combine with the turnips, egg, and egg yolk.
2. Season to taste with salt, pepper, and a little ground ginger. Scale the mixture into 70 g portions.
3. Shape the mixture into a ball then slightly flattened the mixture cakes.
4. Put the mixture through the Standard Breading Procedure. Deep-fry at 180 °C until golden brown.
5. Serve 2 cakes per portion. Accompany with tomato sauce.

Grilled Vegetable Kebabs

Serves:12	Type 1	Prep:12 mins.	Cook: 8-15 mins.

Nutrition per Serving:

50 calories	3 g fat	5 g carbs	1g protein

Ingredients:

- Zucchini (170g, trimmed)
- Yellow Summer Squash (170g, trimmed)
- Bell pepper (170g, red or orange, cut into 4 cm. squares)
- Onion (340g, red, large dice)
- Mushroom caps (12, medium)
- Olive oil (355 ml)
- Garlic (15g, crushed)
- Rosemary (1 ½ tsp, dried)
- Thyme (1/2 tsp, dried)
- Salt (2 tsp)
- Black pepper (1/2 tsp)

Directions:

1. Cut the zucchini and yellow squash into 12 equal slices each.
2. Arrange the vegetables on 12 bamboo skewers. Give each skewer an equal arrangement of vegetable pieces.
3. Place the skewers in a single layer in a hotel pan.
4. Mix the oil, garlic, herbs, salt, and pepper to make a marinade.
5. Pour the marinade over the vegetables, turning them to coat completely.
6. Marinate 1 hour. Turn the skewers once or twice during margination to ensure the vegetables are coated.
7. Remove the skewers from the marinade and let the excess oil drip off.

Vegetable Fritters

Serves:10   Type 1   Prep:15 mins.   Cook: 36 mins.

Nutrition per Serving:

140 calories   6 g fat   19 g carbs   4g protein

Ingredients:

- Egg (3, beaten)
- Milk (230 ml)
- Whole wheat flour (230g)
- Baking powder (1 tbsp)
- Salt (½ tsp)
- Honey (10g)

Vegetables:

- Carrot (340g, diced, cooked)
- Baby lima beans (340g, cooked)
- Asparagus (340g, diced, cooked)
- Celery (340g, diced, cooked)
- Turnip (340g, diced, cooked)
- Eggplant (340g, diced, cooked)
- Cauliflower (340g, diced, cooked)
- Zucchini (340g, diced, cooked)
- Parsnips (340g, diced, cooked)

Directions:

1. Combine the eggs and milk. Mix the flour, baking powder, salt, and honey. Add to the milk and eggs and mix until smooth.
2. Let the batter stand for several hours in a refrigerator. Stir the cold, cooked vegetable into the batter.
3. Drop with a No. 24 scoop into deep fat at 180 ºC. Toss the content from the scoop carefully in the hot oil. Fry until golden brown.
4. Drain well and serve.

Fruit and Nut Snack Mix

Serves:4   Type 1   Prep:10 mins.   Cook: 20 mins.

Nutrition per Serving:

370 calories   12 g fat   64 g carbs   7g protein

Ingredients:
- ❖ Olive oil (1 tbsp.)
- ❖ Honey (70g)
- ❖ Almond extract (1 tsp.)
- ❖ Ground cinnamon (1 tsp.)

- ❖ Old-fashioned oats (470g)
- ❖ Almonds (110g)
- ❖ Dried banana chips (110g)
- ❖ Tropical fruit mix (110g)
- ❖ Raisins (110g)

Directions:
1. Preheat oven to 180 °C. In a saucepan, melt butter. Add honey, almond extract, and cinnamon. Mix well. Add oats and stir.
2. Prepare a baking pan by lining it with parchment paper. Transfer the sticky oat mixture to the baking pan and spread it evenly.
3. It should be no more than about 3 cm thick. Bake for 10 minutes. Stir in almonds and bake for 5 minutes.
4. Remove from the oven. Add the bananas, fruits, and raisins. Cool completely before serving.

Dessert Recipes

Sweet-Baked Banana

Serves:5   Type 1   Prep: 15 mins.   Cook: 20 mins.

Nutrition per Serving:

181 calories   1 g fat   48 g carbs   2g protein

Ingredients:
- ❖ Bananas (6 ripe)
- ❖ Honey (4 tbsp.)
- ❖ Cinnamon (3 ¾ tsp.)

Directions:
1. Preheat oven to 180 °C. Slice bananas into bite-sized chunks.
2. Pour honey and cinnamon into a medium-sized bowl. Mix until cinnamon is evenly spread through the honey.
3. Add bananas and gently toss until they have an even coating.
4. Transfer bananas onto a lined baking sheet. Spread them into one even layer.
5. Place the baking sheet into the oven and bake for 10-15 minutes or until bananas are slightly browned.
6. Portion into 2 bowls and enjoy!

Banana Pudding with Meringue

Serves:10   Type 2   Prep:30 mins.   Cook: 20 mins.

Nutrition per Serving:

324 calories   14 g fat   42 g carbs   12g protein

Ingredients:

For the Pudding:
- ❖ Erythritol (1 ¾ dl)
- ❖ Almond flour (5 tsp.)
- ❖ Salt (¼ tsp.)
- ❖ Fat-free milk (6 dl)
- ❖ Prepared egg replacement (6 tbsp.)
- ❖ Vanilla extract (½ tsp.)

- ❖ Spelt hazelnut biscuits (2 (230g) containers honey-free, crushed)
- ❖ Bananas (5 medium, sliced)

For the Meringue:
- ❖ Egg whites (5 medium)
- ❖ Erythritol (⅔ dl)
- ❖ Vanilla extract (½ tsp.)

Directions:

To Make the Pudding
1. In a saucepan, whisk the erythritol, almond flour, salt, and milk together. Cook over medium heat until the honey is dissolved.
2. Whisk in the egg replacement and cook for about 10 minutes, or until thickened.
3. Remove from the heat and stir in the vanilla. Spread the thickened pudding onto the bottom of a casserole dish.
4. Arrange a layer of crushed biscuits on top of the pudding. Place a layer of sliced bananas on top of the biscuits.

To Make the Meringue
1. Preheat the oven to 180 ºC. In a medium bowl, beat the egg whites for about 5 minutes, or until stiff.
2. Add the erythritol and vanilla while continuing to beat for about 3 more minutes.
3. Spread the meringue on top of the banana pudding.
4. Transfer the casserole dish to the oven, and bake for 7 to 10 minutes, or until the top is lightly browned.

Walnut Crescent Cookies

Serves:10   Type 1   Prep:50 mins.   Cook: 20 mins.

Nutrition per Serving:

408 calories   30 g fat   30 g carbs   6g protein

Ingredients:

Dough:
- ❖ Whole wheat flour (470g)
- ❖ Corn oil (2 ⅓ dl)
- ❖ Dry white wine (1 ⅛ dl)
- ❖ Honey (70g)

Filling:
- ❖ Walnuts (250g, diced)
- ❖ Apple (1, shredded)
- ❖ Honey (2 tbsp.)
- ❖ Whole wheat breadcrumbs (2 tbsp.)
- ❖ Strawberry jam (1 tbsp.)
- ❖ Cinnamon (½ tsp.)
- ❖ Honey for dusting

Directions:

1. Put the corn oil and honey in a large bowl and stir together until well combined.
2. Add the dry white wine and whole wheat flour. Beat this in until a dough is formed.
3. Once dough forms, remove it from the bowl and knead it over a flat surface until soft, but not sticky. Then, let the dough sit for 30 minutes.
4. While the dough sits, you can begin to prepare the filling. Start by putting the walnuts, apple, honey, whole wheat breadcrumbs, strawberry jam, and cinnamon in a large bowl.
5. Mix all the ingredients until well combined. Set aside. Preheat oven to 180 °C.
6. Once half of an hour has passed, flatten the dough out over a floured flat surface until it is 5 mm thick.
7. Using a glass cup, cut circles out of the dough.
8. Set the circles aside, roll the remaining dough out again and repeat step 7 until little or no dough is left.
9. Once all of your dough has been cut into circles, divide the filling between them, dolloping a little bit in the centre of each.
10. Fold each circle in half over the top of the filling and squish the edges nicely into one another so that none of the filling can seep out.
11. Line a baking sheet with parchment paper and spread the crescents out over the top.
12. Place the baking sheet in the oven and let the crescents bake for 20 minutes.
13. After 20 minutes, remove the baking sheet from the oven. Dust with Honey.

Orange Bundt Cake

Serves:24   Type 2   Prep:15 mins.   Cook: 30 mins.

Nutrition per Serving:

180 calories   12 g fat   15 g carbs   4g protein

Ingredients:

- Unsalted non-hydrogenated plant-based butter, for greasing the pan
- Baking flour (350g gluten-free, plus more for dusting)
- Almond flour (350g)
- Baking soda (½ tsp.)
- Baking powder (½ tsp.)
- Eggs (9 medium, at room temperature)
- Coconut honey (220g)
- Zest of 3 oranges
- Juice of 1 orange
- Extra-virgin olive oil (2 ⅓ dl)

Directions:

1. Preheat the oven to 160 °C. Grease two Bundt pans with butter and dust with the baking flour.
2. In a medium bowl, whisk the baking flour, almond flour, baking soda, and baking powder together.
3. In a large bowl, whip the eggs with the coconut honey until they double in size.
4. Add the orange zest and orange juice. Add the dry ingredients to the wet ingredients, stirring to combine.
5. Add the olive oil, a little at a time, until incorporated. Divide the batter between the two prepared Bundt pans.
6. Transfer the Bundt pans to the oven, and bake for 30 minutes, or until browned and a toothpick inserted into the centre comes out clean.
7. Remove the Bundt pans from the oven and let cool for 15 minutes.
8. Invert the Bundt pans onto plates, and gently tap the cakes out of the pan.

Traditional Ekmek Kataifi

Serves:12   Type 1   Prep:30 mins.   Cook: 1 hr. 20 mins.

Nutrition per Serving:

367 calories   20 g fat   45 g carbs   6g protein

Ingredients:

Pastry:
- ❖ Kataifi dough (230g)
- ❖ Pistachios (80g, diced)
- ❖ Olive oil (1 ⅛ dl)

Syrup:
- ❖ Water (1 ¾ dl)
- ❖ Honey (180g)
- ❖ Cinnamon (110 g)
- ❖ Strawberry puree (⅔ dl)

- ❖ Lemon zest (½ tbsp.)

Custard:
- ❖ Milk (7 ⅛ dl, cold)
- ❖ Honey (150g)
- ❖ Olive oil (¾ dl)
- ❖ Corn starch (¾ dl)
- ❖ Egg yolks (4)
- ❖ Vanilla extract (½ tsp.)

Directions:

1. Preheat oven to 170 ⁰C. Knead the Kataifi dough, spreading apart the clumped together strands to create a fluffier consistency.
2. Spray a baking dish with cooking spray and press the Kataifi dough into the bottom of it, forming one even layer.
3. Pour the olive oil over the top and place the baking dish in the oven for 30-40 minutes, or until it is light brown.
4. While the Kataifi is in the oven, you can begin to prepare your custard. Start by placing half of the honey and all the egg yolks in a bowl, whisking them together until well combined and bubbly. Set the mixture aside for later.
5. In a separate bowl, whisk together 4 tbsp. of milk and the corn starch until well combined. Set this mixture aside for later as well.
6. Pour the remaining milk into a large non-stick pan over high heat along with the honey and vanilla extract.
7. Stir this together well and bring the mixture to a boil. Remove the pan from the heat as soon as the milk begins to boil. Set aside.
8. Pour 1/3 of the pan's mixture into the egg yolk mixture and whisk it in until well combined.
9. Transfer the egg yolk mixture back into the pan and place the pan back overheat, but this time on medium.
10. Whisk continuously while cooking is in progress until the mixture becomes all thick, smooth, and deliciously creamy.

11. Once the mixture is thick and rich, remove it again from the heat.
12. Add the olive oil to the pan and stir it into the mixture until melted and well combined.
13. Transfer this mixture into a baking tray and place some plastic wrap over the top of it. Ensure the plastic wrap touches the mixture to ensure it stays creamy.
14. Set this aside, let it cool, and while you're going strong, begin to prepare the syrup.
15. Stir the water, honey, strawberry puree, lemon zest, and cinnamon stick together in a small pot or saucepan over medium heat until the honey has dissolved.
16. Bring the mixture to a boil and let it boil for 3 minutes until it thickens into a syrup consistency.
17. Once it's thick enough, remove it from the heat and let it cool until it's just warm enough for you to eat it without burning your mouth.
18. By now your Kataifi dough should have been removed from the oven and cooled. If this is not the case, wait until it is cool.
19. Once the Kataifi is cool, ladle the syrup over the top one at a time, giving each spoonful enough time to be absorbed. Then, set it aside to cool completely.
20. Spread the creamy custard atop the Kataifi in a nice, even layer.
21. Sprinkle the chopped pistachios over the entire thing. You can be as creative as you like!
22. Make a smiley face or a rainbow to impress your friends.
23. Slice into 12 pieces, serve, and enjoy!

Flaky Coconut Pie

Serves:12	Type 1	Prep:30 mins.	Cook: 45 mins.

Nutrition per Serving:

385 calories	28 g fat	31 g carbs	6g protein

Ingredients:

- Filo pastry (11 sheets)
- Coconut cream (400 ml)
- Cashew (1 ⅛ dl, chopped)
- Honey (110g)
- Coconut oil (80g)
- Coconut (80g, shredded, unsweetened)
- Eggs (2)
- Vanilla extract (1 tsp.)

Directions:

1. reheat oven to 180 °C. Grease a pie dish with just enough coconut oil to cover it.
2. In a medium-size bowl, whisk together the coconut cream, honey, eggs, and vanilla until all ingredients are well combined and the honey has dissolved. Set this aside for later.
3. Pulse the cashews and shredded coconut in a food processor until it turns into mulch. Set this aside as well.
4. Place a piece of the filo pastry on a clean, stable surface and brush a generous amount of coconut oil over it.
5. Roughly scrunch the piece of filo pastry up and place it in the pie dish. Repeat steps 5-6 until the baking tray is full.
6. Once your pie dish is full, pour the coconut cream mixture over top, making sure each inch of the pastry gets soaked in it.
7. Once you're out of your coconut cream mixture, sprinkle the cashew mixture over top.
8. Place the pie dish in the oven and let it bake for 25-35 minutes or until the top has turned a nice golden-brown and the pastry has risen.
9. Remove the baking tray from the oven and allow your pie to cool for 15 minutes.
10. Slice into 8 wedges and enjoy!

Ricotta Cheese Fruit Bake

Serves:6   Type 1   Prep:30 mins.   Cook: 1 hr.10 mins.

Nutrition per Serving:

153 calories   6 g fat   19 g carbs   8g protein

Ingredients:

Ricotta Cheese:

- ❖ Ricotta cheese (350g)
- ❖ Egg (1)
- ❖ Honey (3 tbsp.)
- ❖ Lemon zest (1 tsp.)

Fruit Syrup:

- ❖ Raspberries (250g, diced)
- ❖ Honey (3 tbsp.)
- ❖ Orange juice (2 tbsp.)
- ❖ Orange blossom water (1 tsp.)

Directions:

1. Place ricotta cheese in a coffee filter-lined strainer and place this in the fridge to drain overnight.
2. Ensure the filter is placed over a container so that the drained mixture is contained.
3. Once your ricotta cheese has drained, preheat the oven to 200 °C. Spray 6 small heat-proof bowls with cooking spray.
4. Place the drained ricotta, egg, honey, and lemon in a bowl and beat together until well combined.
5. Divide the ricotta mixture between your 6 greased bowls and place them in the oven for 30-35 minutes, or until they have turned a nice golden-brown colour.
6. Then, remove them from the oven and allow them to cool. While your ricotta cheese bowls are cooling, you can begin to prepare the fruit sauce.
7. Start by placing the raspberries, honey, and orange juice in a small pot or saucepan over medium-high heat.
8. As it starts to boil, stir so that ingredients are well combined and the honey dissolves.
9. Once the mixture starts to boil, reduce the heat to medium-low and continue to cook, stirring occasionally, for 20-25 minutes or until the raspberries are tender and the mixture takes on a syrupy consistency.
10. Remove the mixture from the heat and stir in the orange blossom water until well combined. Then, let the mixture cool a little.
11. Once the ricotta cheese bowls have cooled, divide the fruit syrup over them.
12. Serve and enjoy!

Anginetti Lemon Cookies

Serves:12   Type 1   Prep:30 mins.   Cook: 20 mins.

Nutrition per Serving:

104 calories   3 g fat   18 g carbs   1g protein

Ingredients:

Cookies:
- ❖ Whole wheat flour (150g)
- ❖ Egg (1)
- ❖ Honey (2 ½ tbsp.)
- ❖ Olive oil (2 tbsp.)
- ❖ Baking powder (2/3 tsp.)
- ❖ Vanilla extract (2/3 tsp.)
- ❖ Lemon zest (1/3 tsp., grated)

Icing:
- ❖ Honey (110g, sifted)
- ❖ lemon juice (2 tsp.)
- ❖ water (2 tsp.)
- ❖ olive oil (1 tsp.)
- ❖ vanilla extract (1/3 tsp.)

Directions:

1. Preheat oven to 180 ᵒC. Prepare a baking sheet by lining it with foil.
2. Start with the cookies. Beat together the honey, olive oil, vanilla extract, and lemon zest together until ingredients are well combined.
3. Crack the egg into the mixture and beat it in as well. Then, set this mixture aside for later.
4. In a separate bowl, stir together the whole wheat flour and baking powder until well combined.
5. Gradually add this to the wet mixture, beating it in as you go.
6. Once your cookie dough is smooth and lump-free, begin to dollop it out onto the lined baking sheet. You should be able to get 12 cookies out of the mixture.
7. Place the baking sheet into the oven and bake for 10-12 minutes or until they become a nice golden-brown colour.
8. While the cookies are in the oven, you can begin to prepare the icing. Start by putting the olive oil in a small pot or saucepan over medium heat.
9. Once the oil has heated, add in the honey, lemon juice, water, and vanilla extract, stirring ingredients into the oil until well combined. Add a little more water to the icing if it seems too thick.
10. Once the cookies are done, brush the lemon icing over the top while they're still hot.
11. After you have applied the icing, allow the cookies to cool.
12. Once the cookies are cool, serve, and enjoy!

Banana, Peach, and Almond Fritters

Serves:7   Type 2   Prep:15 mins.   Cook: 15 mins.

Nutrition per Serving:

163 calories   7 g fat   22 g carbs   6g protein

Ingredients:

- Bananas (4 ripe, peeled)
- Peaches (470g, chopped)
- Egg (1 medium)
- Egg whites (2 medium)
- Almond meal (180g)
- Almond extract (¼ tsp.)

Directions:

1. In a large bowl, mash the bananas and peaches together with a fork or potato masher.
2. Blend in the egg and egg whites. Stir in the almond meal and almond extract.
3. ⅔-dl portions of the batter into the basket of an air fryer. Set the air fryer to 200 °C. Close, and cook for 12 minutes.
4. Once cooking is complete, transfer the fritters to a plate. Repeat until no batter remains.

Toasted Almond Biscotti

Serves: 20   Type 1   Prep: 20 mins.   Cook: 35 mins.

Nutrition per Serving:

74 calories   3 g fat   11 g carbs   3g protein

Ingredients:

- Whole wheat flour (300g)
- Honey (110g)
- Almonds (80g, toasted and chopped)
- Eggs (2 small)
- Egg wash (1 small egg, beaten with ½ tbsp. Water)
- Sesame seeds (2 ½ tbsp., toasted)
- Orange flower water (1 tbsp.)
- Anise seeds (1 tsp.)
- Baking powder (¾ tsp.)
- Vanilla extract (½ tsp.)
- Almond extract (¼ tsp.)

Directions:

1. In a medium-sized bowl, mix the almond extract, honey, orange flower water, almonds, vanilla extract, anise seeds, and 2 tbsp. sesame seeds until well combined.
2. Once all ingredients are well combined, crack the 2 eggs into the mixture and beat them in until thoroughly distributed.
3. Gradually beat in the flour and baking powder until a dough form. Place this dough in the fridge to cool for 30 minutes.
4. Now, preheat oven to 180 °C. Coat your hands and a clean, stable surface with flour and knead the dough into a rectangular loaf.
5. Transfer this loaf to a baking sheet and brush the egg-water over it until the entire loaf is covered.
6. Then, coat the outside with your remaining sesame seeds.
7. Place the loaf in the oven and let it bake for about 15 minutes, or until it begins to turn a light gold colour.
8. Transfer the loaf from the oven to a cooling rack. Leave to cool for about 15 minutes. Don't turn the oven off!
9. Once your loaf is cool enough to touch, slice it into 20 pieces and arrange them, cut side down, on another lined baking sheet.
10. Place the baking sheet back in the oven and let the biscotti's bake for another 15-20 minutes, or until they have turned a nice golden-brown colour.
11. Remove the baking pan from the oven, let the cookies cool, and enjoy with some tea or coffee!

Greek Rice Pudding

Serves:12   Type 1   Prep:15 mins.   Cook: 35 mins.
Nutrition per Serving:

52 calories   2 g fat   8 g carbs   2g protein

Ingredients:
- Full-fat milk (5 ½ dl)
- Rice (3 tbsp.)
- Honey (3 tbsp.)
- Corn flour (½ tbsp.)
- Cold water (1 tsp.)

Directions:
1. Put a pot with the milk over medium-high heat and cook until it comes to a boil.
2. Reduce the heat to medium-low and stir in the rice and honey until well combined. Keep stirring until the honey is completely dissolved.
3. Once the honey has dissolved, turn the heat down to low and let the mixture cook for 20-30 minutes, or until the rice has cooked.
4. Once the rice is cooked and tender, mix the corn flour and water in a small bowl until a smooth yet runny paste forms. Use more water if needed.
5. Add the corn flour mixture to the pot and stir it in until well combined.
6. Let the pudding simmer, stirring constantly, until it reaches your desired consistency.
7. Remove from heat, divide between two bowls, and serve!

Orange and Peach Ambrosia

Serves:8 Type 2 Prep:10 mins. Cook: 0 mins.

Nutrition per Serving:

113 calories 5 g fat 12 g carbs 2g protein

Ingredients:

- Oranges (3, peeled, sectioned, and quartered)
- Peaches (4 diced in water, drained)
- Unsweetened coconut (230g, shredded)
- Crème fraîche (1 (230-g) container fat-free)

Directions:

1. In a large mixing bowl, combine the oranges, peaches, coconut, and crème fraîche.
2. Gently toss until well mixed. Cover and refrigerate overnight.

Avocado Mousse with Grilled Watermelon

Serves:8 Type 2 Prep:10 mins. Cook: 10 mins.

Nutrition per Serving:

127 calories 4 g fat 24 g carbs 3g protein

Ingredients:

- Watermelon (1 small, seedless, halved and cut into 3-cm rounds)
- Avocados (2 ripe, pitted and peeled)
- Plain yogurt (110g, fat-free)
- Cayenne pepper (¼ tsp.)

Directions:

1. On a hot grill, grill the watermelon slices for 2 to 3 minutes on each side, or until you can see the grill marks.
2. To make the avocado mousse, in a blender, combine the avocados, yogurt, and cayenne and process until smooth.
3. To serve, cut each watermelon round in half. Top each with a generous dollop of avocado mousse.

Zucchini and Pinto Bean Casserole

Serves:4   Type 2   Prep:15 mins.   Cook: 15 mins.
Nutrition per Serving:
251 calories   12 g fat   23 g carbs   16g protein

Ingredients:
- ❖ Zucchini, (1 large, trimmed)
- ❖ Non-stick cooking spray
- ❖ Pinto beans (1 can, 430-g)
- ❖ Salsa (200g)
- ❖ Mexican cheese blend (240g, shredded)

Directions:
1. Slice the zucchini into rounds. You'll need at least 16 slices. Spray a 15-cm cake pan with non-stick spray.
2. Put the beans into a medium bowl and mash some of them with a fork.
3. Cover the bottom of the pan with about 4 zucchini slices. Add about ⅓ of the beans, ⅓ cup of salsa, and ⅓ cup of cheese. Press down. Repeat for 2 more layers. Add the remaining zucchini, salsa, and cheese. (There are no beans in the top layer.)
4. Cover the pan loosely with foil.
5. Pour 2 ⅓ dl of water into the electric pressure cooker.
6. Place the pan on the wire rack and carefully lower it into the pot. Close and lock the lid of the pressure cooker. Set the valve to sealing.
7. Cook on Manual/Pressure Cook for 15 minutes.
8. When the cooking is complete, hit Cancel and allow the pressure to release naturally.
9. Once the pin drops, unlock and remove the lid.
10. Carefully remove the pan from the pot, lifting by the handles of the wire rack. Let the casserole sit for 5 minutes before slicing into quarters and serving.

Vegetable Enchilada Casserole

| Serves:6 | Type 2 | Prep:15 mins. | Cook: 15 mins. |

Nutrition per Serving:

| 172 calories | 7 g fat | 21 g carbs | 8g protein |

Ingredients:

- Extra-virgin olive oil (1 tbsp.)
- Onion (½ medium, chopped)
- Garlic cloves (3, minced)
- Green bell pepper (½, deseeded and chopped
- Red bell pepper (½, deseeded and chopped)
- Zucchinis (2 small, chopped)
- Enchilada sauce (1 can 280 g, low sodium)
- Black beans (1 can 430 g, low sodium, drained and rinsed)
- Ground cumin (1 tsp.)
- Cheddar cheese (110g shredded, divided)
- Corn tortillas (2, cut into strips)
- Salt (¼ tsp.)
- Black pepper (¼ tsp., freshly ground)
- Coriander (chopped fresh, for garnish)
- Plain yogurt, for serving

Directions:

1. Preheat the broiler to high. Heat the olive oil in a large ovenproof skillet until it shimmers.
2. Stir in the onion, garlic, bell peppers, and zucchinis and sauté for 3 to 5 minutes, or until the onion is translucent.
3. Add the enchilada sauce, black beans, cumin, ⅔ dl of cheese, tortilla strips, salt, and pepper and whisk to combine. Scatter the top with the remaining ⅔ dl of cheese.
4. Place the skillet under the broiler and broil until the cheese melts, 5 to 8 minutes.
5. Sprinkle the coriander on top for garnish and serve topped with the yogurt.

Tomato, Lentil and Chickpea Curry

Serves: 6   Type 2   Prep: 10 mins.   Cook: 25 mins.

Nutrition per Serving:

340 calories   8 g fat   50 g carbs   18g protein

Ingredients:

- ❖ Extra-virgin olive oil (1 tbsp.)
- ❖ Sweet onion (1, chopped)
- ❖ Garlic (1 tsp., minced)
- ❖ Fresh ginger (1 tbsp., grated)
- ❖ Red curry paste (2 tbsp.)
- ❖ Turmeric (½ tsp.)
- ❖ Cumin (1 tsp., ground)
- ❖ Cayenne pepper (pinch)

- ❖ Lentils (470g, cooked)
- ❖ Tomatoes (800g can, low sodium, diced)
- ❖ Chickpeas (430g can water-packed, rinsed and drained)
- ❖ Coconut milk (⅔ dl)
- ❖ Fresh coriander (2 tbsp., chopped)

Directions:

1. Heat the olive oil in a large saucepan over medium-high heat.
2. Add the onion, garlic, and ginger and sauté for about 3 minutes until tender, stirring occasionally.
3. Stir in the red curry paste, turmeric, cumin, and cayenne pepper and sauté for another 1 minute.
4. Add the cooked lentils, tomatoes, chickpeas, and coconut milk and stir to combine, then bring the curry to a boil.
5. Once it starts to boil, reduce the heat to low and bring to a simmer for 20 minutes.
6. Serve garnished with the coriander.

Cheesy Quinoa Casserole

Serves: 4   Type 2   Prep: 20 mins.   Cook: 30 mins.

Nutrition per Serving:

305 calories   9 g fat   38 g carbs   17g protein

Ingredients:

- Extra-virgin olive oil (1 tsp.)
- Sweet onion (½, chopped)
- Garlic (2 tsp. Minced)
- Eggs (2, whisked)
- Quinoa (450g, cooked)
- Cherry tomatoes (480g)
- Ricotta cheese (120g, low-fat)
- Salt (to taste)
- Ground black pepper (to taste)
- Zucchini (1, cut into thin ribbons)
- Pine nuts (30g, toasted)

Directions:

1. Preheat the oven to 180 ºC. Heat the olive oil in a medium skillet over medium-high heat.
2. Sauté the onion and garlic for 3 minutes, stirring occasionally, or until softened.
3. Remove the skillet from the heat. Add the whisked eggs, cooked quinoa, cherry tomatoes, and cheese and stir to incorporate.
4. Sprinkle with salt and pepper. Transfer the mixture to a baking dish.
5. Sprinkle the top with the zucchini ribbons and pine nuts. Bake in the preheated oven for about 25 minutes, or until the casserole is heated through.
6. Cool for 5 to 10 minutes before serving.

Zoodles with Beet and Walnut Pesto

Serves:2	Type 2	Prep:20 mins.	Cook: 40 mins.

Nutrition per Serving:

424 calories	39 g fat	17 g carbs	8g protein

Ingredients:

- Red beet (1 medium, peeled, chopped)
- Extra-virgin olive oil (2 tsp.)
- Walnut pieces (10, toasted)
- Goat cheese (110g, crumbled)
- Garlic cloves (3)
- Lemon juice (2 tbsp., freshly squeezed)
- Extra-virgin olive oil (2 tbsp.)
- Salt (¼ tsp.)
- Zucchini (4 small, spiralized)

Directions:

1. Preheat the oven to 190 ºC. Wrap the red beet in aluminium foil, making sure to seal the foil completely.
2. Roast in the preheated oven for 30 to 40 minutes until tender.
3. When ready, transfer the red beet to a food processor. Fold in the toasted walnut, goat cheese, garlic, lemon juice, 2 tablespoons of olive oil, and salt and pulse until smooth.
4. Transfer the beet mixture to a small bowl. Heat the remaining 2 teaspoons of olive oil in a large skillet over medium heat.
5. Add the zucchini, tossing to coat in the oil. Cook for 2 to 3 minutes, stirring constantly, or until the zucchini is softened.
6. Remove the zucchini from the heat to a plate and top with the beet mixture. Toss well and serve warm.

Pita Stuffed with Tabbouleh

Serves:4   Type 2   Prep:20 mins.   Cook: 0 mins.

Nutrition per Serving:

245 calories   8 g fat   39 g carbs   7g protein

Ingredients:

- Bulgur wheat (230g, cooked)
- English cucumber (1, finely chopped)
- Yellow bell pepper (1, deseeded and finely chopped)
- Cherry tomatoes (480g, halved)
- Fresh parsley (110g, finely chopped)
- Scallions (2, white and green parts, finely chopped)
- Juice of 1 lemon
- Extra-virgin olive oil (2 tbsp.)
- Salt (to taste)
- Ground black pepper (to taste)
- Whole-wheat pitas (4, cut in half)

Directions:

1. Combine the bulgur wheat, cucumber, bell pepper, tomatoes, parsley, scallions, lemon juice, and olive oil in a large bowl and stir to mix well. Season with salt and pepper to taste.
2. Place the pita halves on a clean work surface. Evenly divide the bulgur mixture among pita halves and serve immediately.

Egg and Pea Salad in Kale Wraps

Serves:2   Type 2   Prep:10 mins.   Cook: 0 mins.

Nutrition per Serving:

296 calories   18 g fat   18 g carbs   17g protein

Ingredients:

- Eggs (4 hard-boiled large, chopped)
- Peas (210g fresh, shelled)
- Red onion (2 tbsp., finely chopped)
- Sea salt (½ tsp.)
- Paprika (¼ tsp.)
- Dijon mustard (1 tsp.)
- Fresh dill (1 tbsp., chopped)
- Mayonnaise (3 tbsp.)
- Kale leaves (2 large)

Directions:

1. Combine all the ingredients, except for the kale leaves, in a bowl. Stir to mix well.
2. Divide and spoon the mixture on the kale leaves, then roll up the leaves to wrap the mixture. Serve immediately.

Beef and Mushroom Barley Soup

| Serves:6 | Type 2 | Prep:10 mins. | Cook: 1 hr.20 mins. |

Nutrition per Serving:

| 245 calories | 9 g fat | 19 g carbs | 21g protein |

Ingredients:

- Beef stew meat (450g, cubed)
- Salt (¼ tsp.)
- Ground black pepper (¼ tsp.)
- Extra-virgin olive oil (1 tbsp.)
- Mushrooms (230g, sliced)
- Onion (1, chopped)
- Carrots (2, chopped)
- Celery stalks (3, chopped)
- Garlic cloves (6, minced)
- Dried thyme (½ tsp.)
- Beef broth (9 ½ dl low sodium)
- Water (3 dl)
- Pearl barley (120g)

Directions:

1. Season the meat with the salt and pepper. In an Instant Pot, heat the oil over high heat.
2. Add the meat and brown on all sides. Remove the meat from the pot and set aside.
3. Add the mushrooms to the pot and cook for 1 to 2 minutes, until they begin to soften.
4. Remove the mushrooms and set aside with the meat. Add the onion, carrots, and celery to the pot.
5. Sauté for 3 to 4 minutes until the vegetables begin to soften. Add the garlic and continue to cook until fragrant, about 30 seconds longer.
6. Return the meat and mushrooms to the pot, then add the thyme, beef broth, and water.
7. Set the pressure to high and cook for 15 minutes. Let the pressure release naturally.
8. Add in your barley. Close the lid and use the slow cooker setting. Continue cooking for 1 hour until the barley is cooked through and tender. Serve.

Hearty Corn on the Cob

Serves:12	Type 2	Prep:10 mins.	Cook: 20 mins.

Nutrition per Serving:

64 calories	1 g fat	14 g carbs	2g protein

Ingredients:

❖ Corn (6 ears)

Directions:

1. Remove the husks and silk from the corn. Cut or break each ear in half.
2. Pour 1 cup of water into the bottom of the electric pressure cooker. Insert a wire rack or trivet.
3. Place the corn upright on the rack, cut side down. Close and lock the lid of the pressure cooker.
4. Set the valve to sealing. Cook on Manual/Pressure Cook for 5 minutes.
5. When the cooking is complete, hit Cancel and quick release the pressure.
6. Once the pin drops, unlock and remove the lid. Use tongs to remove the corn from the pot.
7. Season as desired and serve immediately.

Garlicky Broccoli Florets

Serves:8	Type 2	Prep:10 mins.	Cook: 25 mins.

Nutrition per Serving:

33 calories	2 g fat	3 g carbs	1g protein

Ingredients:

- Broccoli heads (2 large, cut into florets)
- Extra-virgin olive oil (2 tbsp.)
- Garlic cloves (3, minced)
- Salt (¼ tsp.)
- Ground black pepper (¼ tsp.)
- Freshly squeezed lemon juice (2 tbsp.)

Directions:

1. Preheat the oven to 220 °C and line a large baking sheet with parchment paper.
2. In a large bowl, add the broccoli, olive oil, garlic, salt, and pepper. Toss well until the broccoli is coated completely. Transfer the broccoli to the prepared baking sheet.
3. Roast in the preheated oven for about 25 minutes, flipping the broccoli halfway through, or until the broccoli is browned and fork tender.
4. Remove from the oven to a plate and let cool for 5 minutes. Serve drizzled with the lemon juice.

Mushroom Tofu Stew

Serves:2	Type 2	Prep:15 mins.	Cook: 10 mins.

Nutrition per Serving:

180 calories	11 g fat	5 g carbs	34g protein

Ingredients:

- mushrooms (500g chopped)
- tofu (500g chopped)
- mushroom soup (250 ml)
- mixed herbs (1 tbsp.)
- onion (1 minced)

Directions:

1. Mix all the ingredients in your Instant Pot.
2. Cook on Stew for 10 minutes.
3. Release the pressure naturally.

Egg And Chicken Stew

Serves: 2   Type 2   Prep: 15 mins.   Cook: 10 mins.

Nutrition per Serving:

340 calories   20 g fat   10 g carbs   43g protein

Ingredients:

- Chicken (450g cooked, shredded)
- Vegetables (500g, chopped)
- Broth (250 ml, low sodium)
- Eggs (2 hard boiled, quartered)
- Herbs (1 tbsp., mixed)

Directions:

1. Mix all the ingredients in your Instant Pot.
2. Cook on Stew for 10 minutes.
3. Release the pressure naturally.

Shrimp Chowder

Serves: 2   Type 2   Prep: 15 mins.   Cook: 10 mins.

Nutrition per Serving:

270 calories   15 g fat   10 g carbs   35g protein

Ingredients:

- Shrimp (450g, cooked)
- Vegetables (450g, chopped)
- White sauce (250 ml)
- Herbs (1 tbsp, mixed)

Directions:

1. Mix all the ingredients in your Instant Pot.
2. Cook on Stew for 10 minutes.
3. Release the pressure naturally.

Bread Pudding with Kale and Mushrooms

Serves: 2   Type 2   Prep: 20 mins.   Cook: 20 mins.

Nutrition per Serving:

296 calories   17 g fat   23 g carbs   13g protein

Ingredients:

- Egg (1 large)
- 2% milk (1 ⅛ dl)
- Dijon mustard (½ tsp.)
- Nutmeg (pinch, freshly grated)
- Kosher salt (pinch)
- Ground black pepper (pinch)
- Sourdough bread (1 slice, about 30 g, cut into 3-cm cubes)
- Avocado oil (1 tbsp.)
- Onion (150g chopped)
- Mushrooms (60g, sliced, about 3 creminis)
- Dried thyme (¼ tsp.)
- Lacinato kale (220g chopped, stems and ribs removed from 2 stems)
- Non-stick cooking spray
- Gruyere cheese (100g, grated)
- Parmesan (1 tbsp., shredded)

Directions:

1. In a 4-¾-dl measuring cup with a spout, whisk together the egg, milk, mustard, nutmeg, salt, and pepper.
2. Add the bread and submerge it in the liquid. Set the electric pressure cooker to the Sauté setting.
3. When the pot is hot, pour in the avocado oil. Add the onion, mushrooms, and thyme to the pot and sauté for 3 to 5 minutes or until the onion begins to soften.
4. Stir in the kale and cook for about 2 minutes or until it wilts. Hit Cancel.
5. Spray the ramekins with cooking spray. Divide the mushroom mixture between the ramekins.
6. Top each with 2 tablespoons Gruyere. Pour half of the egg mixture into each ramekin and stir.
7. Make sure the bread stays submerged. Cover with foil.
8. Pour 2 ⅓ dl of water into the electric pressure cooker and insert a wire rack or trivet. Place the ramekins on the rack.
9. Close and lock the lid of the pressure cooker. Set the valve to sealing.
10. Cook on Manual/Pressure Cook for 8 minutes. When the cooking is complete, hit Cancel.
11. Allow the pressure to release naturally for 10 minutes, then quick release any remaining pressure.
12. Using tongs or the handles of the rack, transfer the ramekins to a cutting board.
13. Carefully lift the foil and sprinkle the Parmesan on top. Replace the foil for about 5 minutes or until the cheese melts.
14. Remove the foil and serve immediately.

Pumpkin Soup

| Serves:2 | Type 2 | Prep:15 mins. | Cook: 10 mins. |

Nutrition per Serving:

| 200 calories | 11 g fat | 7 g carbs | 2g protein |

Ingredients:
- Pumpkin (450g, chopped)
- Tomato (450g, chopped)
- Broth (250 ml)
- Herbs (1 tbsp., mixed)
- Onion (1, minced)

Directions:
1. Mix all the ingredients in your Instant Pot.
2. Cook on Stew for 10 minutes.
3. Release the pressure naturally.
4. Blend.

Irish Lamb

| Serves:2 | Type 2 | Prep:15 mins. | Cook: 10 mins. |

Nutrition per Serving:

| 450 calories | 27 g fat | 10 g carbs | 41g protein |

Ingredients:
- lamb (500g, cooked, chopped)
- cabbage (500g, shredded)
- beer (250 ml, low carb)
- herbs (1 tbsp., mixed)
- onion (1, minced)

Directions:
1. Mix all the ingredients in your Instant Pot.
2. Cook on Stew for 10 minutes.
3. Release the pressure naturally.

Simple Parmesan Acorn Squash

Serves:4   Type 2   Prep:10 mins.   Cook: 20 mins.

Nutrition per Serving:

86 calories   4 g fat   12 g carbs   2g protein

Ingredients:

- acorn squash (1, about 450g)
- extra-virgin olive oil (1 tbsp.)
- sage leaves (1 tsp. dried, crumbled)
- nutmeg (¼ tsp., freshly grated)
- kosher salt (⅛ tsp.)
- ground black pepper (⅛ tsp.)
- Parmesan cheese (2 tbsp., freshly grated)

Directions:

1. Cut the acorn squash in half lengthwise and remove the seeds. Cut each half in half for a total of 4 wedges.
2. Snap off the stem if it's easy to do. In a small bowl, combine the olive oil, sage, nutmeg, salt, and pepper.
3. Brush the cut sides of the squash with the olive oil mixture.
4. Pour 2 ⅓ dl (240 g) of water into the electric pressure cooker and insert a wire rack or trivet.
5. Place the squash on the trivet in a single layer, skin-side down. Close and lock the lid of the pressure cooker.
6. Set the valve to sealing. Cook on Manual/Pressure Cook for 20 minutes.
7. When the cooking is complete, hit Cancel and quick release the pressure.
8. Once the pin drops, unlock and remove the lid.
9. Carefully remove the squash from the pot, sprinkle with the Parmesan, and serve.

Clam Chowder

Serves: 2   Type 2   Prep: 15 mins.   Cook: 10 mins.

Nutrition per Serving:

300 calories   3 g fat   4 g carbs   42g protein

Ingredients:
- Shelled clams (500g cooked)
- Vegetables (500g chopped)
- White sauce (250 ml)
- Herbs (1 tbsp., mixed)
- Onion (1, minced)

Directions:
1. Mix all the ingredients in your Instant Pot.
2. Cook on Stew for 10 minutes.
3. Release the pressure naturally.

Eggs And Sausage

Serves: 2   Type 2   Prep: 15 mins.   Cook: 7 mins.

Nutrition per Serving:

210 calories   15 g fat   3 g carbs   22g protein

Ingredients:
- Eggs (3)
- Milk (⅔ dl)
- Sausage (250g, chopped, cooked)
- Bacon (110g, chopped, cooked)
- Pinch of salt

Directions:
1. Spray a heat-proof bowl that fits in your Instant Pot with non-stick spray. Whisk together the eggs, milk, and salt.
2. Pour into the bowl. Add the sausage and bacon. Place the bowl in your steamer basket.
3. Pour 2 ⅓ dl of water into your Instant Pot.
4. Lower the basket into your Instant Pot. Seal and cook on low pressure for 7 minutes. Depressurize quickly.
5. Stir well and allow to rest, it will finish cooking in its own heat.

Pork And Mushrooms

Serves:2   Type 2   Prep:15 mins.   Cook: 10 mins.

Nutrition per Serving:

410 calories   20 g fat   10 g carbs   42g protein

Ingredients:
- Pork (500g, cooked, diced)
- Mushrooms (500g, chopped, mixed)
- Mushroom soup (250 ml)
- Herbs (1 tbsp., mixed)
- Cheddar (1 tbsp., shredded)

Directions:
1. Mix all the ingredients in your Instant Pot.
2. Cook on Stew for 10 minutes.
3. Release the pressure naturally

BLOOD SUGAR LOG

	TIME	BEFORE	AFTER	NOTES
Monday	Morning			
	Noon			
	Afternoon			
	Before sleep			
Tuesday	Morning			
	Noon			
	Afternoon			
	Before sleep			
Wednesday	Morning			
	Noon			
	Afternoon			
	Before sleep			
Thursday	Morning			
	Noon			
	Afternoon			
	Before sleep			
Friday	Morning			
	Noon			
	Afternoon			
	Before sleep			
Saturday	Morning			
	Noon			
	Afternoon			
	Before sleep			
Sunday	Morning			
	Noon			
	Afternoon			
	Before sleep			

	TIME	BEFORE	AFTER	NOTES
Monday	Morning			
	Noon			
	Afternoon			
	Before sleep			
Tuesday	Morning			
	Noon			
	Afternoon			
	Before sleep			
Wednesday	Morning			
	Noon			
	Afternoon			
	Before sleep			
Thursday	Morning			
	Noon			
	Afternoon			
	Before sleep			
Friday	Morning			
	Noon			
	Afternoon			
	Before sleep			
Saturday	Morning			
	Noon			
	Afternoon			
	Before sleep			
Sunday	Morning			
	Noon			
	Afternoon			
	Before sleep			

	TIME	BEFORE	AFTER	NOTES
Monday	Morning			
	Noon			
	Afternoon			
	Before sleep			
Tuesday	Morning			
	Noon			
	Afternoon			
	Before sleep			
Wednesday	Morning			
	Noon			
	Afternoon			
	Before sleep			
Thursday	Morning			
	Noon			
	Afternoon			
	Before sleep			
Friday	Morning			
	Noon			
	Afternoon			
	Before sleep			
Saturday	Morning			
	Noon			
	Afternoon			
	Before sleep			
Sunday	Morning			
	Noon			
	Afternoon			
	Before sleep			

	TIME	BEFORE	AFTER	NOTES
Monday	Morning			
	Noon			
	Afternoon			
	Before sleep			
Tuesday	Morning			
	Noon			
	Afternoon			
	Before sleep			
Wednesday	Morning			
	Noon			
	Afternoon			
	Before sleep			
Thursday	Morning			
	Noon			
	Afternoon			
	Before sleep			
Friday	Morning			
	Noon			
	Afternoon			
	Before sleep			
Saturday	Morning			
	Noon			
	Afternoon			
	Before sleep			
Sunday	Morning			
	Noon			
	Afternoon			
	Before sleep			

	TIME	BEFORE	AFTER	NOTES
Monday	Morning			
	Noon			
	Afternoon			
	Before sleep			
Tuesday	Morning			
	Noon			
	Afternoon			
	Before sleep			
Wednesday	Morning			
	Noon			
	Afternoon			
	Before sleep			
Thursday	Morning			
	Noon			
	Afternoon			
	Before sleep			
Friday	Morning			
	Noon			
	Afternoon			
	Before sleep			
Saturday	Morning			
	Noon			
	Afternoon			
	Before sleep			
Sunday	Morning			
	Noon			
	Afternoon			
	Before sleep			

	TIME	BEFORE	AFTER	NOTES
Monday	Morning			
	Noon			
	Afternoon			
	Before sleep			
Tuesday	Morning			
	Noon			
	Afternoon			
	Before sleep			
Wednesday	Morning			
	Noon			
	Afternoon			
	Before sleep			
Thursday	Morning			
	Noon			
	Afternoon			
	Before sleep			
Friday	Morning			
	Noon			
	Afternoon			
	Before sleep			
Saturday	Morning			
	Noon			
	Afternoon			
	Before sleep			
Sunday	Morning			
	Noon			
	Afternoon			
	Before sleep			

	TIME	BEFORE	AFTER	NOTES
Monday	Morning			
	Noon			
	Afternoon			
	Before sleep			
Tuesday	Morning			
	Noon			
	Afternoon			
	Before sleep			
Wednesday	Morning			
	Noon			
	Afternoon			
	Before sleep			
Thursday	Morning			
	Noon			
	Afternoon			
	Before sleep			
Friday	Morning			
	Noon			
	Afternoon			
	Before sleep			
Saturday	Morning			
	Noon			
	Afternoon			
	Before sleep			
Sunday	Morning			
	Noon			
	Afternoon			
	Before sleep			

Thank you for going through the book, I sincerely hope you enjoyed the recipes.

As I said before, a lot of time went into creating so many recipes and I really hope you're satisfied with the recipes provided.

I'm trying really hard to create the best recipes I can and I'm always open to feedback so whether you liked or disliked the book feel free to write on my email at deliciousrecipes.publishing@gmail.com. I always reply and love to communicate with everybody. If you didn't like the recipes you can reach out and I'll share another cookbook or two for free in order to try to improve your experience at least a little bit.

Thank you for going through the recipes, enjoy!

Printed in Great Britain
by Amazon

18063100R00091